The Demon Cat of Calle del Rio

A year in a
Spanish mountain village

Best wishes.

Art Lester

23 Nov 2014

ISBN: 978-1-326-05519-6

PublishNation, London
www.publishnation.co.uk

Chapter One

The End of the World

When Ellen and I set out on a brief visit to an old friend, we expected the travel to be challenging. After all, that remote Spanish valley known as the Alpujarras has been isolated and all but cut off from history by steep mountains and treacherous roads. A glance at a map would have suggested a journey of two or three hours. We couldn't have known that ours was to last more than a year.

It began when a train ironically called *El Expreso* pulled into the station at Guadix late on a Sunday afternoon. The journey from Barcelona had taken nearly eighteen hours. Because of works on the line near Albacete, we had been diverted through Murcia and then on a snail-like passage through one of the driest areas of Spain. The six of us strangers occupying a triple-decker sleeping compartment had been through all the stages of temporary relationship: shyness, followed by overly-animated conversation (if you counted the pidgin Spanish of my wife and me), then by fatigue and recrimination as others snored, tossed and sweated the short night away. By the time we arrived in Guadix, all of us simply wanted the journey to be over. Unfortunately, as we were soon to realise, the real travel was just about to begin.

We were alone as we stepped on to the platform, except for a comatose guard in a straight-backed chair against an unattended kiosk. On the station forecourt hung a sign for a taxi rank, but there wasn't a single car to be seen. At this late hour we were casting long shadows on the dusty pavement. Though we knew more or less where we wanted to go, we hadn't a clue where we were. Ellen sat on the large suitcase and we shared the last of a bottle of water. We hadn't been in Spain very long, but already we had learned what to do next: wait.

After half an hour I was beginning to worry. We had arranged to meet our friend Bill sometime this afternoon in the village to which he had recently moved, and the afternoon was quickly vanishing. I decided to leave the station compound to look for some sign of life when a taxi pulled on to the forecourt. It didn't come near the taxi rank, but parked in the shade of the only tree in sight about fifty yards away. As my bad Spanish was allegedly the better of the two of us, I went to speak to him. He was a slight man with greasy, thick-lensed glasses and a black tobacco cigarette dangling from his lip. I put my head into the passenger side window, but before I could speak he wagged his index finger at me in that way that resembles a windscreen wiper, signifying, "no."

"We want to go to Latigos," I said. The driver continued to wag. He was squinting at me as if over a great distance.

"Latigos," I repeated. "Please."

He shook his head and uttered something that I could tell was probably perfectly reasonable, though I didn't catch a word. I persisted, putting aside embarrassment, because I didn't know what else to do.

"Latigos," I said again. "*Por favor.*"

A long moment passed, during which I could intuit that his frustration level was equal to my own. It was a Mexican stand-off. I had decided that unless he actually drove away I was going to keep smiling and insisting. I could feel Ellen rooting for me from the taxi rank. Finally, with an air of resignation, he reached forward and started the engine. I tightened my grip on the window. He motioned for me to get in. I pointed to Ellen and he nodded, putting the car into reverse and squealing his tires as he pulled up in front of her. We loaded the bags ourselves.

We were off, me sitting protectively in the front and Ellen behind, surrounded by luggage. Once outside the station enclosure, I could see that we were in a flat fertile valley bordered by limestone cliffs. The slanting rays of the sun etched shadows that emphasised the folds of the cliffs. We jolted off down a perfectly straight blacktop highway toward what I came to know as the north face of the Sierra Nevada, a vast, looming presence turning purple in the waning light. The driver was hurrying, and although there was no traffic in either direction, the ageing, badly-sprung Renault was lurching and bouncing on the road surface. I had a fleeting image of us upside down in the dry fields to the side of us, wheels spinning in the air, horn blaring crazily a la final scenes in Hollywood B movies. To distract myself more than anything else, I mustered my best Spanish and asked which way we were going. The driver jabbed a nicotine-darkened finger up at the mountains.

"Is it very far?" I asked.

He said something in reply and laughed. I couldn't catch his meaning. I looked around at Ellen.

"I think he said, 'It's the end of the world,'" she muttered.

At the foot of the only route over the eastern Sierra Nevada there is a castle, known as La Calahorra. It sits atop a small hill by itself, devoid of vegetation. You would recognise it immediately, since it has featured in half a dozen films and television commercials. Built toward the end of the sixteenth century, it is still the property of a Spanish count and his family. At the foot of the hill there are some houses and a bar for the few travellers who risk the route over the mountain pass called La Ragua. Without a word, the driver pulled over, parked and went inside. Ellen and I got out and looked around. The mountains loomed like an uncertain fate. We reassured ourselves that, though they looked impossibly high, there was probably an element of illusion involved. Our friend Bill had always been a fairly reasonable sort, and we were sure that he wouldn't lead us somewhere dangerous. Or so we said to each other, beginning, after the heat of the day, to shiver in the gathering twilight.

After what seemed an unreasonably long time the driver reappeared. As he passed I smelled alcohol on his breath and realised that he had been having his Sunday afternoon drink inside, passengers or no passengers. Ellen didn't seem to notice. I looked around at the bar, at the castle, at the few cars parked outside the sparse settlement and made a decision: better to risk the road ahead than try to find our own way from here in the dark. With a leaden feeling, I got in and we took off up the mountain road.

At first the ascent to La Ragua is gradual. The road has been widened in recent years and visibility around bends is good. But at this time, before the European Union investment in rural roads, the pavement was cracked and broken at the edges. The gradual ascent gives way without warning to tight u-bends and blind corners. Sitting on the curb side, I soon noticed that I could look directly down at sheer drops of a hundred feet or so. The driver was going faster that I thought

4

sensible, but my poor Spanish and a sense of inevitability made me keep my dry mouth shut. Tires squealed. Headlamps bounced off rocks and trees, then shone into emptiness as we rounded bends. The angle of ascent pressed us back against our seats. For the first time I noticed a large plastic crucifix was dangling from the rear view mirror. The driver smoked and stared straight ahead, occasionally cursing when the road narrowed or fallen rocks lay in the road.

As we climbed the temperature dropped. The driver shrugged on a jacket without stopping. I kept one hand ready to grab the wheel when it surely would become necessary. The light was almost gone, but as we manoeuvred through a particularly sharp switchback I looked down and saw the castle, at least a thousand feet below. It was like looking from the window of an airplane. I decided not to point this out to Ellen, but when I looked back at her I could see her eyes, round and white in the gloom.

"Latigos," said the driver and gave a bitter, perhaps drunken, laugh. "Latigos." At first I thought he was announcing our arrival, but we were still ploughing uphill, hugging the inside of a road that the mountain was clearly trying, with small landslides and eroded edges, to shrug off. I realised that he was making some ironic commentary of his own, fuelled by the *aguardiente* he had consumed ten miles back and several thousand feet below us.

Up we went through plantations of pine and patches of *encina*, the Iberian evergreen oak. Fallen rocks ranging from fist to watermelon size appeared in the headlamps. The driver swerved with what I considered to be undue nonchalance. Suddenly my ears popped, and as I raised my hand to massage my jaw I realised that I had been gripping the door handle so tightly that my fingers ached. It was as if my body had been ignoring my brain and was ready to jump at any second.

5

A last long rise ended in what must have been the first flat stretch of road since La Calahorra. We shot through a notch in the stone face onto a kind of narrow mountain meadow bordered on both sides with steep slopes leading up to unseen heights. We passed a sign that announced we were in Puerto de la Ragua, altitude 1995 meters. I calculated that this meant more than 6,000 feet, a mile and a quarter in the air. This was the pass over the Sierra Nevada, the only one until you reach Granada. It was cold, even in the car. For the first time we saw the moon, about half full. It lit up the landscape with small glints of reflection off the granite walls and droplets of condensation in the trees. A momentary feeling of happiness surprised me, as I realised that we might actually survive this excursion into the unknown, and that, even if we didn't, we had picked a supremely beautiful place to die.

From there we started downhill again. A road sign said that we were thirty kilometres from someplace called Cherin. It was comforting even though we'd never heard of the place, as if the mere existence of road markers meant the road had at least been previously travelled by someone else. The road was wider and the curves more sweeping. Each time we made an outside curve I could see over a range of hills below to the reflection of the moon on what had to be the sea. Lulled into a kind of pleasant semi-coma by the sweep of the curves, I was startled by the sight of a village apparently just a few yards away. I sat up and, pointing, asked, "Latigos?"

The windscreen wiper gesture again, accompanied by a grunt. The driver pointed down along the road, meaning we would have to descend some more. The lights of the village seemed to be floating in the air. As we rounded a bend I saw why. As a crow might see it, the village of Bayarcal was only a mile or two away. But a road sign at the edge of a rocky dirt road said it was some ten miles. I realised that in order to get there one would have to drive down to the bottom of a valley and up the other side, a journey of over an hour in these parts, though you could practically wave to someone in the plaza from this road. Bayarcal rose gradually above us as we descended through land that had begun to look more agricultural than wild. I could pick out a few trees that looked like chestnuts, and there were a few rows of almonds and figs.

We were unprepared for the sight of Latigos when it came. We rounded a bend and saw three old buildings on the edge of a steep slope which disappeared again as we passed a road sign saying *"Terminal Muncipio de Latigos."* Again we were in open country, and I was about to ask the driver if we had passed the place by when another bend led us onto a road at the top of a town tumbling below us precariously into the blackness. Again we appeared to leave sight of the place and enter open country, and again a bend brought us to lights and buildings. I realised that the village was built on a slope so steep that it was necessary to wind in and out of the village to get to the bottom of it. One last curve and we found ourselves in a broad stretch of pavement with what seemed to be a park built on the edge of the mountain.

"Latigos," said the driver, this time with finality. He did not stop the engine, but extended his hand for payment. I shovelled pesetas at him, not caring how much it cost. I felt the gratitude of an astronaut returning to earth. We got out under a lone street light next to a couple of parked vans. Across the road we could see something that looked like a store next to several houses. The driver turned and sped back up the way we had come. I realised now why he had been so reluctant to make the trip. If I had known I would have thought twice myself.

"Well," I said. "Looks like the end of the line."

"Or the end of the world," Ellen grumbled.

Chapter Two

Public Inconvenience

Bill had said, "Just meet me in the Plaza. I'll be there late afternoon, but if I'm not, just ask for me. I'm the only foreigner in town—everybody knows me."

Fine, except we didn't know where the Plaza was, and there was nobody to be seen. It was dark outside of the pale circle of the street lamp and it was biting cold. We rummaged in our luggage and found jumpers and put them on with stiffening fingers. Even though it was only October, the air at three thousand feet chilled the blood. I could see my breath like cigarette smoke in the gloom. And I had another little problem. I needed what the English call a "public convenience."

That was easily solved. It was pitch black outside the feeble ring of light cast by the street lamp. I told Ellen to wait and shuffled carefully into the little park, bumping into a couple of stone benches and making my way to a low stone wall. Below me there seemed to be a drop like those on the road up here, hundreds of feet of cold darkness. There were no lights to be seen. I looked over my shoulder before proceeding and then relieved myself into the darkness with the sneaky delight of a schoolboy. Suddenly there was the sound of furious barking and the unmistakable sound of living beings stirring a few feet below. Many beings, just below my feet. I hurried back to our perch on the road with a red face that I hoped Ellen wouldn't see. So far things weren't going to plan.

The barking died down. I decided that the dimly lit doorway across the paved area was some kind of public establishment. Leaving Ellen with the bags I went across, rousing several more dogs in nearby houses. There was a dim light over a doorway three steps down from street level. The door was ajar. I could hear the sound of female voices. Steeling myself, I swept aside a ceramic bead curtain and pushed the door open, smacking my head on the lintel as I did.

A short woman in a black dress was standing behind a refrigerated box laden top and bottom with foodstuffs. A dim light bulb was the only illumination. Strings of sausages hung from overhead and all around her were laden to groaning shelves of tinned goods, flyswatters and mops, dolls and insect sprays, spatulas and espadrille sandals. On my side of the counter were two other women, wedged between open boxes of fruits and vegetables set on the stone floor. I was on one foot against a bucket in which hoes and shovels were splayed against the wall.

Nobody looked at me. Their conversation had stopped, but the woman behind the counter went on stacking sausages onto a piece of waxed paper. One of the customers studied the ceiling while the other kept her eyes on the floor. I cleared my throat and smiled, but there was no response. The proprietor said something in a low voice to one of her customers as she wound the packet of sausages with string.

"Excuse me very much," I said ungrammatically, earning the briefest of glances from the owner, but she turned her attention to the other customer who began calmly to unfold a shopping list.

"I'm looking for Bill," I said in Spanish I had been practising all the way to Latigos. Bill is six-two, so I raised my hand a few inches over my head. "Bill," I said, "Amigo."

The woman looked at me as if observing some phenomenon from a wildlife television programme. I could see that this was not meant unkindly, but was evidence that, whatever I might be, I was just too strange to be taken seriously. She asked the customer something under her breath. The other shook her head.

I began one of those elaborate pantomimes that anyone who has ever been without the language in a foreign country will recognise. I dramatically re-created the drive up the mountains with an invisible steering wheel, turning it extravagantly back and forth and making motor noises at the same time. The women stopped and stared while I mopped my brow, indicating fatigue and folded my head on my hands in a gesture representing sleep. I pointed to the door and indicated that my wife was outside in the cold, saying "*Mujer. Mujer.*" Further emphasising the point, perhaps unwisely, I made hourglass figure curves with my hands.

"Bill, *amigo*," I said, warming to the task. He was fair-haired, so I reached into my scanty bag of Spanish words. "*Alto* (tall) *rubio* (blond)."

The women looked at each other. The customer sniggered; the owner scowled.

"*Aqui, no.*" she said sharply, "*Nada de eso.*" Her patience seemed to be coming to an end. She came around from behind the counter, small but intimidating. Her face was stern and her posture showed that she knew she was in charge. The hilarity of the other was infecting her as well, though. I could see that.

10

Maybe they were starting to like me. I pointed to the door, indicating the Ellen was waiting outside, and said again, pleading, "*Mujer. Mujer.*"

The owner made broom-like gestures with her hands, as if shooing away flies.

"*Vayase al bar,*" she said loudly, sweeping me toward the door, "*Bar. Bar.*"

Even with my high school Spanish I could gather that she was sending me to the bar, wherever that was. I went halfway through the door and she shoved one thick arm past me, gesturing to the left. I went through and pointed elaborately in the direction she had indicated.

"*Bar?*" I asked, and happy to be communicating at last, said it again twice more. She stood back before closing the door, her face more pitying than unkind. It seemed that my attempt at communication had been less than successful.

Ellen was sitting with her arms wrapped around herself against the cold when I got back. Her eyes asked the question. I was too embarrassed to share the gory details of my failed encounter with Latigos, so I put the best possible face on things.

"No problem," I said. "Bill's waiting in the bar."

You can find a bar in any Spanish village. This is not because the Spanish are particularly alcoholic, but because the bar is more than just a place to get booze. It is the one place where messages can be relayed, resources found, bills paid, mail collected. It is where children buy their ice cream and people pick up their packages left by the taxi driver on his return from the city. It is where women stand in the doorway while the barman fills 2-litre plastic Pepsi bottles with dinner wine from a barrel. If you are going to find Bill at all, you will find him there.

We dragged the suitcases through streets that were hardly wide enough for a car. The white-fronted houses we passed all

11

looked tightly shut against the dark and cold. We heard low voices from inside and occasionally smelled cooking, reminding us that it had been eight hours since we had shared a *chorizo* sandwich on the train. We nearly walked right past the Bar Nevada, as I later learned it was called, because there was no sign marking its existence. The door stood open onto the street and there was a faint murmur of conversation. Otherwise it looked exactly like any other building in town. We took deep breaths and went in.

The Bar Nevada had a floor covered with sawdust and wood shavings, piled so deeply in places that you could trip if you weren't careful. There was only one source of light, a bare 25-watt bulb swinging over the stone counter. Men were pressed against the bar, dozens of them with stubby glasses of red wine and glowing cigarettes. There was an area beyond of such darkness that it could have contained anything, like the entrance to the underworld. But there was no sign of Bill.

All conversation stopped dead. No one stared at us. In fact I had the same eerie sensation that I had had upon entering the shop that I had become, if not invisible, then drastically irrelevant. Ellen stayed behind me, more aware than I was that there wasn't a single woman to be seen. I took the bull by the horns.

"*Buenas noches*," I said in the direction of the barman, a thickset man with strands of thinning hair combed over his pate. Everyone seemed to nod without actually speaking. I felt that we were being observed outside the line of our vision, and that if I turned rapidly enough I would catch people watching slack-jawed with amazement. They were, however, as I was to learn later, too polite and hospitable to stare openly.

"*Buena noche*," the barman replied. Rural Andalucians rarely bother with final esses.

Encouraged, I tried, "I'm looking for Bill."

There was no spark of recognition from the barman. I didn't know whether this was due to my bad Spanish, or if, by some horrible mischance, we had landed up in the wrong village.

"Bill," I tried again. I raised my hand to six inches above my head. "*Alto. Rubio. Extranjero.*"

Still nothing. I could feel Ellen's spirits sag behind me. A short man in a cloth cap detached himself from the bar. He approached and dragged two chairs from a nearby table and gestured for us to sit down. He said something to the barman, who served up two glasses of the strong local wine. With it came two *tapas*, small legs of recently shot pheasant in a rich wine sauce and two hunks of bread. I leaned against the table and drank a goodly slug. Ellen tucked into the pheasant without a word. The nourishment hit me with a warm glow. We said nothing until the food and wine were gone. I noticed that conversation had resumed. The short man was standing by us with an amused expression. He re-ordered and we did not complain. This time there were strips of white fish and red peppers and more bread. Life was beginning to seem possible.

The short man leaned over and put a horned finger on my breastbone in a gentle but insistent way. He had the kind of eyes that are said to twinkle, and in the years that followed I would get to know them well.

"Bee," he said.

"Huh? I mean, *que?*"

He raised his hand over his head just as I had done, and said again, "Bee."

It occurred to me that the sound of Bill's name as we would pronounce it has no equivalent in Spanish. It would be pronounced "Bee."

"Yes, Bee," I laughed, looking at Ellen, "Bee. Bee!"

The man gestured with his head and I turned to see Bill leaning in the doorway, grinning. Ellen rushed up and kissed him. I maintained my reserve, draining the last of my wine before grabbing his hand.

"I thought I'd better come and get you," he said, "before you make even worse fools of yourselves."

He introduced us to the short man, whose name was Aparicio. We shook hands and I made an apologetic gesture of sleep. He nodded and we left the Bar Nevada, forgetting even to pay for our drinks. But that's usual in the Sierra Nevada: even if I'd remembered, someone else would have hospitably insisted on paying the tab. It's just the way things are around there.

In a few minutes we had drunk another couple of glasses of wine, in Bill's little village house, swapped stories and settled down in a creaky overstuffed bed with a pile of blankets. Ellen was fading, but just before I drifted into sleep I called to Bill in the other room,

"What did you mean when you said 'before we make worse fools of ourselves'?"

"Well, Art," came Bill's droll tones out of the dark, "I can't begin to imagine what Rosario in the shop was thinking, what with your, um, Spanish, except that you seemed to be asking her to find you a woman." He chuckled, not unkindly. "But what possessed you to piss on her husband's sheep?"

Chapter Three

Absentees and Other Landlords

By now, Ellen and I were getting used to waking up in strange beds. There had been the deep, quilt-covered sanctuary of the draughty house in Sussex, where we spent a year training for work in rural villages of the poor world. Then the Spartan metal cots of our rondavel in Botswana, where we worked with the gentlest people we had ever met under a relentless African sky. Innumerable *charpoys* in India, where we made sandaled pilgrimages and fought off dysentery, and all the hotels, hostels, temporary accommodation in training centres and in cities whose exotic names still filled me with excitement: Nairobi, Johannesburg, Bombay, Bulawayo. We had learned to ignore the confusion of opening our eyes to unknown ceilings of crumbling plaster and thatch, to lie still until the logic of location reasserted itself.

This morning, we awoke in amazement. Light was streaming down a staircase onto our bed from Bill's open attic. I went up into this room, designed for hanging chillies to dry and storing maize for the animals. One end of the house was open to the front except for a low railing.

Across the rooftops of the houses Latigos tumbled away down towards a river, which was marked by the tops of poplar trees. On the opposite bank were terraces made of un-mortared stone rising like stairs to the crest of a hill, each planted with crops or olive trees. The air was ice-clear. The most distant sights took on a blue tint, like early Renaissance paintings. In a fold of the mountains opposite the river wound through a pass toward the sea, shining now in the morning sun like a sheet of glass. Involuntarily I caught my breath and turned to see Ellen, wrapped modestly in a bedspread, with the same look of reverent astonishment I must have worn myself.

Down at street level mules and horses were being led from the corrals under the houses by men in working clothes. A few women could be seen on the flat rooftops, hanging up washing. They didn't seem to be, as we were, stunned by the vista before us. A boy on a motorbike sped furiously past the pack animals, leaving a trail of exhaust fumes and a terrible racket in the narrow street. On distant terraces early risers could be seen moving about slowly, and down by the river a small troop of workers and horses moved sedately in the still shaded valley. I tried to remember what I had read about this place in the travel books.

Las Alpujarras is a valley some sixty miles long that lies between the high peaks of the Sierra Nevada and a lower coastal range, the Contraviesa. Until recently it was one of the poorest and most isolated regions of Spain. Counting every small settlement, there are about a hundred villages tucked into the creases or hung off the slopes of the mountains. The villages are unique architecturally, consisting of flat roofed houses waterproofed with *launa*, a local fine clay. To find anything similar you would have to go to the Berber villages in Morocco.

This was the last stronghold of the Moors when they were driven out by the Catholic kings. There was active Moorish resistance for nearly a century after Granada fell in 1492. The land is steep and rugged. Agriculture takes place in those few spots where irrigation can be used, and to accomplish this, the Moors built a system of *acequias*, or irrigation canals, that have endured until the present day. These begin high on the slopes where springs from the melting mountains snows flow to the surface and lead down, clinging to sheer cliff faces and cut through solid rock as much as three thousand feet to arable land below. So complex is this system, and so skilled were the Moorish engineers, that the Catholics grudgingly allowed two families to remain in each village after the conquest, to manage the irrigation. The rest were converted to Christianity or expelled, replaced by immigrants from far away places like Galicia. But over the years, the Moors slipped back into the valley, intermarried and formed the *Morisco*, the unique culture of the Alpujarras.

At one time the hillsides were covered in plantations of mulberry shrubs, which produced silkworms and fed the local silk factories. According to local historians, the last silk factory in the town of Ugijar closed in the early part of the twentieth century after over 800 years of production. It is said that silk at one time made the coastal town of Adra, founded by the Phoenicians, the second busiest port in the western Mediterranean. Today you can still see mulberries clinging to the margins of the tilled land, although they are considered troublesome encumbrances to agriculture and often cut down.

As in many hillside agricultural areas, the fertile slopes are terraced with stones laid without mortar, creating small patches of land flat enough to grow crops. It is not possible to till these pockets of soil with machinery because of difficulty of access, and so, even today, there is a widespread use of mules and horses, the manure of which fertilises the land. In some ways little has changed from the time of the Moors.

One day Ellen and I woke up and realised that we were in a rut. For the first ten years of our marriage we had focussed on making money. We had succeeded, more or less. The restaurant opened by a couple of wide-eyed novices in had grown and then multiplied into a franchise company. Losing patience with commerce, we had sold out and bought a few beach apartments in a South Carolina resort town. We had some money in the bank, a steady income earner, and loads of free time. We weren't rich, but we didn't have to count pennies, either.

But there was just too much free time. After jogging a couple of miles each morning, there was virtually nothing left to do. We read a lot, walked on the beach, cooked wonderful dinners and watched television. I tried golf and tennis, but it just wasn't me. After six months I was pacing the floor like a captive animal. I was still in my mid-thirties, and retirement seemed more like punishment than reward.

One day we got word of a training program in England, teaching skills to benefit people in rural areas of the Third World. It offered courses in small-scale agriculture, nutrition and appropriate technology. Compared to our small comfortable world, England sounded wonderfully exotic. Within three months we had sold up, banked the money and moved to a small village in East Sussex. Eighteen months after that, we were in a Botswana village.

You get used to things more easily than you expect. The people you work with are poor, and there is more than anyone's fair share of hardship. Things like a lack of running water and electricity can be endured, and even enjoyed. There is no TV, but there is sky—such sky as demands to be watched—and people who sit in their doorways and talk until bedtime, who have real neighbours, so that they don't need soap operas. There are new problems: you substitute malaria for stickups in the local 7-Eleven. Ellen and I had gradually grown to love a world that wasn't known about back home. Our roots, if not severed, were getting thinner. This was worrying, but the compensations of this rootless existence, at least so far, were sufficient.

As we stood in Bill's attic that morning, I felt the same opening up of my senses that I had felt in Botswana. The look on Ellen's face showed that she felt it too. Dark-haired and slightly almond-eyed, she carried a genetic hint of bloodlines that may have sprung from some Mediterranean land like this one. In Spanish-speaking cultures, people always addressed their words to her, since my Anglo-Saxon features seemed the less likely to afford comprehension. She was not tall, but, as she herself said, sturdy. She joked that she was the kind of earth mother that could "drop a baby in the fields and keep on working with one hand." She had the kind of face you wanted to rest your eyes on. I had, without complaint, for more than ten years.

Of the two of us, she was the more cautious. She was an artist and a musician, and carried all the sensitivity that these callings suggest. My risk-taking nature was a contrast, but one that she seemed to have accepted. When I sometimes asked her about it, she would smile wryly and say, "You know, man, 'whither thou goest' and all that." But she sometimes seemed bewildered with my need to keep moving, changing environments, as she said, like socks.

She made coffee and we drank it in the *camara*, reluctant to leave the sight of the Alpujarra's morning. Bill had left us a note saying he was going to the *campo* with Aparicio, and leaving us instructions on how to join them. He had told us that he was renovating a small farm he had bought further down the hillside and that Aparicio was helping him get started. The *finca* was called Cortijo El Gitano, and his note said, I thought somewhat kindly, that we couldn't miss it as it was down the main highway from Latigos in the direction of the sea.

We set out, passing through the small park or *paseo* where the taxi driver had left us last night. It was a pretty little half circle built on a terrace beside the entrance to the village, with a fountain and a ring of cypress trees. I looked over the wall and saw a roofless stone shelter built beneath it that was clearly meant to hold sheep, something I had already gathered. There was no one about, which was good, since I wouldn't have been able to explain myself anyway.

We went down the blacktop road past a row of houses built on a ledge with gardens below. It was easy to see where there was water, since nearly all vegetation in the eastern Alpujarra depends on irrigation. The grass by the roadside was dry and yellowed after the long summer just past, but where cultivation was possible, everything was green and lush. There were small patches of vegetables interplanted with olive trees and almonds, whose furry pods were beginning to turn dry. Some apples and pears looked ready for picking, and young oranges were green in the dark-leafed trees. Almost as an afterthought, wide-branching half-wild fig trees hugged the margins of the terraces. The sun was hot overhead, and we peeled off a layer of clothing as we descended.

Bill's note had told us to keep to the road until we came to an old stone gate across the road with the remains of an iron arch above it. After a half hour's walk there was no sign of a gate. We were travelling along the edge of a steep gorge that led down to a river which we could hear but not see. The opposite side of the gorge was unpopulated and dry, with sisal plants and prickly pears clinging to the slope among huge boulders. We passed through a cut in the rocks where only one car at a time could pass and saw ahead of us wider, flatter terraces planted with grapevines on a gradual slope to the flat land by the river. On a ridge, ringed with terraces, we spotted a yellow house with a chimney. Two figures and a horse moved about in a field.

"That's Bill," I said, pointing.

"How do you know?" Ellen asked, having recent reason to doubt my navigational skills.

"Because he's taller than anybody else around here. Look how much shorter the other guy is. Anyway, it would be just like him to paint his house a different colour from everybody else."

"The gate's got to be pretty close, then."

"I don't think we need to go as far as the gate," I said. "Look at this path. It goes down along the side and cuts out that next curve. Come on, let's see."

"No way, Hawkeye. I'm following directions until I know where I am."

"Chicken."

"Chicken, maybe, but I'm sticking to the road. You try the path if you want."

Maybe it was her tone of voice, or maybe I wanted to get even for the times in the past twenty-four hours when I had made a fool of myself. I wasn't sure the path would get to Bill's house at all, although I couldn't imagine why not. I was tempted, but bit my lip and followed her down the road. Later I would realise that, taking the small trail, I would have wound up scratched, muddy and humiliated, in the river.

Bill's house was a converted *cortijo* , a small building made of stone where farmers store the tools and crops they need at the land. As in many Mediterranean cultures, people lived together in villages, where there was water and transport and—above all—company, then commuted each day to the fields. The rural areas of the Alpujarras are dotted with these small stone buildings.

Bill had extended his by adding a room where there had been a porch. It was now two rooms with new concrete floors and some glass for the small windows. The house stood on a broad terrace overlooking the steep river gorge that marked the boundary of village property. Across the gorge the land was too steep to cultivate until a level almost with the village Bayarcal we had seen the night before. It was cliff-like, with jutting boulders and stalky sisal plants and cactus. Bill's land went most of the way to the river, becoming increasingly steeper until it reached a dense, almost sunless wood.

The river was more like what people in moister climates would call a stream. At its widest no broader than a rural road, it ran through tumbled rocks and fallen trees to a depth of never more than a metre. But it had the advantage of having no upstream neighbours. It rose in a *nacimiento*, or spring, halfway up the dry slope to Bayarcal and fell sharply over a thousand metres, even creating small *chorros*, or waterfalls, on its way. And it was clean enough to drink. The only possible pollutants upstream would be the manure of a stray goat or the remains of a rabbit uncollected by vultures. The people around there did drink it. We would later swim in it many times. You hung most of your clothes on a branch and waded in to knee level, then sat as rapidly as you could into the stream, freezing even in summer, but glorious anyway.

Aparicio rode off on his horse to perform one of the many errands he had as what I would have to call an agricultural consultant. Landless himself, he was in constant demand by other farmers in the valley because of his almost uncanny skill of knowing what to do with plants and creatures. He and Bill had been planning the plantation of the garden surrounding his house. This was to involve hitherto unknown things in this valley: pergolas, lily pond, even herbaceous borders. People were already talking about the farm in the village and were wondering just what was about to happen at Cortijo El Gitano.

Chapter Four

Prickly Pears

Ellen and I huddled. We decided to change our plans. We had intended to spend an extra night in Barcelona, but neither of us wanted to make a move just yet. The Alpujarras had begun to get to us, and for a few moments I regretted that the next year of our lives was already arranged. We had agreed to do a short-term contract in a rural development project in the Dominican Republic, working alongside some old friends from our training days in England. One of our reasons for coming to Latigos, apart from visiting Bill, was to test our Spanish, since we were assured that no one where we were going could speak

English. So far, as they say, no good. I was going to have to knuckle down with the books and audio cassettes, and do it quick, since we were due to start in about a week.

Bill had no language problem, and I envied him. The child of an American father and a Venezuelan mother, he had grown up in Caracas before going to high school in Miami. He spoke English like an American and Spanish like a native, too. We had met a few years before, when he had grown tired of a middling career as a rock and roll singer in Madrid and decided to pursue the natural life. He had been living in Formentera, the smallest of the Balearics, while we were there on an extended holiday. The island at first was undiscovered by tourists, but within a few years had become a destination for the tourist companies from Britain, so that it was fast becoming possible to eat fish and chips and find cans of baked beans in the supermarket. He sold his house, which he had built by hand, and followed rumours to this place, which he felt confident would never be discovered. It was just too remote and too mountainous for that, or so he hoped. So far he was the only foreigner in Latigos.

The house he was occupying belonged to an in-law of Aparicio. No one had as yet got around to charging him rent during his six-month occupancy, though he had decided to pay anyway. He had bought the land with his farmhouse about three months earlier, for such an unbelievably small sum that I had to ask him to repeat the price. Not only was it a good piece of land, but it had road access, something rare in these hills. There were twelve terraces, including four planted with mature olive trees. He planned to harvest these this year and promised to save us a bottle of first press oil.

Bill had an errand to run in Ugijar, the market town that served as a hub for the local villages. He offered to take the scenic route to give us a treat. We squeezed into his 2CV and took off to the west along a flat but treacherously curved road.

25

We drove along the breast of the Sierra for several miles. We could see the whole of the Contraviesa across the valley, where white villages huddled among patches of green fields in the severe brown landscape. Over the mountaintops we could see the flat sheen of the Mediterranean reflecting the sun's ascent. On a clear day, said Bill, the residents of Latigos claimed to be able to see the Atlas Mountains in Morocco, though he never had.

About two miles out of Latigos we caught sight of a church on a bluff above the road. A few metres on we saw a sign that announced the hamlet of Jubar. Bill turned in and we climbed along a tree-shaded road into one of the smallest villages I had ever seen. A dozen or so houses, a few buildings used for agricultural storage, and, at the end of the short road, a huge church. It seemed very grand for such a small place, and I said so. Bill told us that the Church had formerly been very powerful in the region, so much so that a lot of the churches in small places like this were nearly covered inside with gold leaf. The building must have been designed to seat five hundred or so, in a village with a maximum population of fifty. It was more of a symbol of wealth and importance than a functional structure, a sign of the now vanished influence of organised religion in the post-Franco era.

As we left the village Bill told us a story. A few years before, a pair of Japanese newlyweds had arrived unexpectedly in Jubar. They drove a rented car with two fancy bicycles strapped to the roof. They spoke no Spanish, so when they began knocking on doors, reading out of a phrasebook, no one knew what to do with them. After much effort, involving asking for the translation services of a visiting priest, it emerged that they would like to spend some time in the village, cycling and enjoying the sights. They needed accommodation. A large empty house was found and duly cleaned by the owner, a widow who lived in Ugijar. Papers were produced and a visit to a *notario* was organised.

The price of the house, in 1981, was 75,000 pesetas, about six hundred dollars at the existing rate of exchange. The widow was pleased with the price, as it was higher than the average. The Japanese smiled and forked over the money without quibble. They walked and cycled and greeted everyone politely for a month. Their lights could be seen at night, but during the day they were mostly out in the countryside. Until one day the village woke to find them gone.

They left a note in English, which had to be translated by a schoolteacher from Granada, thanking the owner of the house for her hospitality and promising to contact her next time they wanted to visit the valley. They had never been seen since.

"They thought the money was rent," Bill chuckled. "They never dreamed they had bought the place. Now it's empty and nobody knows how to get in touch with them. Every time somebody foreign goes near the village, they get asked if they know so-and-so, because everybody seems to think all foreigners know each other."

Somewhere, in Yokohama or Tokyo, there is a pair of homeowners whose roof needs attention. If you are reading this, please get in touch.

We continued along the breast of the Sierra past Mairena, along a road with bends that Bill swore were more than a hundred and eighty degrees, to the pretty village of Mecinilla, where we turned downhill into a long stretch of curves leading through dense olive groves. People could be seen irrigating their land from the *asequias*, hoeing the earth to allow the water to cover the ground to a depth of several inches. Rounding a bend we saw something incongruous—a large billboard in English offering farms and village houses for sale. A red arrow pointed to a newly constructed office with plate glass windows and parking bays. Bill speeded up and flew past with a grim expression. I asked what that was about.

"It's this Argentinean guy, named Roberto. I knew him in Formentera. He's bad news."

"What's this about selling farms and all?"

Bill smiled wryly. "So far there are hardly any foreigners around here. This guy's a crook. He advertises in British newspapers, promising the moon. When somebody contacts him, he arranges for them to come out. He puts them up in a hotel in Granada and then drives them around the countryside, supposedly showing them *fincas* and houses that are for sale. He makes up a price, a large one. If somebody bites, he gets a deposit from them of ten percent. Then he buys the property from the owner himself and sells it on to the sucker for a thousand percent mark up."

"Do people fall for it?"

"He's sold three or four places, mostly in Mecinilla and Valor," he pointed to the west." They love it because it's romantic and scenic and all, but mostly they don't stay, because they can't understand what anybody says and they find themselves in places with no doctors or drugstores, or even newspapers. Roberto will sell your farm for you, or so he says, but meanwhile he charges a fee to look after the property." Bill smiled ironically. "They don't sell very fast."

"Is he doing that in Latigos?" Ellen asked.

"Not so far. He came up once and Aparicio showed him a *finca* that nobody wants because it's dry. A horsefly bit him. Roberto says it's too primitive for his customers. Let's hope it stays that way."

We came into Ugijar along an avenue of plane trees that had recently been pollarded back to the trunks. They looked a little forlorn, like a man after a bad haircut. Bill said they did that every year after the fiesta, but that by next summer the street would be covered in shade again. There were more cars in the street than we had seen higher up the mountain. There was an air of busyness, though not a lot of hurry. We parked in front of a bar in a patch of shade.

Ugijar was a town, meaning it had a petrol station, a pharmacy, a doctor's surgery, shoe shops and a single hotel with a grand front built up against an eroded earth bank. It was the nearest place to Latigos where you could buy a newspaper, too. Bill left us to stroll around while he went to deal with the electricity company.

We found a public telephone agency near the central square. There were only three phones in Latigos, and using them wasn't always possible. We went through a fly curtain into a foyer with an overstuffed sofa. A girl showed us to a private cabin with two chairs and a black old-style telephone hanging on the wall. We gave her the number we wanted—a travel agent in Malaga Bill had given us-- and after much waiting, got into contact with an English-speaking voice who was able to make a flight reservation for us back to London. Barcelona would have to wait; our train tickets hadn't cost all that much anyway.

We sat in the square for a while, letting the sun bathe us into drowsiness. We watched as a man tried to hitch a donkey to a small cart, while a little girl cried and fretted beside him. The animal wouldn't co-operate, so the man gave the donkey a half-hearted punch to the head. It didn't seem to notice, and after a while the man carried the wailing child inside the house.

We met Bill in the bar after the agreed hour had passed. It was just lunchtime, and people were beginning to file in. It was a high-ceilinged place with bare walls except for an out-of-date calendar and a framed picture of a statue of the Virgin of Pilar with a look of anguish on her face. The barman was a thickset man of middle age with a sour expression. As was the custom all over the Alpujarras, you got free *tapas* every time you ordered a drink. This had to be beer or wine, although a non-alcoholic "wine," really grape juice, also qualified. We ordered three of these and the barman slammed a plate of battered and fried aubergines in front of us. He said nothing, and Bill just nodded. The food was delicious.

"That's Paco El Chumbo," Bill said under his breath. "Chumbo means prickly pear. He's the sourest character in Andalucía. Never been seen to smile. If the tapas weren't so good nobody would ever come in here." We re-ordered and the Chumbo produced grilled sardines and olives. We drank more grape juice and gobbled the delicacies.

"There's a kind of joke around here," Bill said. "It goes that if you can make Chumbo smile then the Virgin in the picture will, too."

"He can't be that bad," I said.

"Go ahead. Try." Bill dared me.

I re-ordered grape juice. The Chumbo brought us three miniature pork steaks with slabs of bread. I smiled at him.

"Thank you very much, sir," I said in rehearsed Spanish and gave my most winning smile. The Chumbo didn't even grunt.

I wasn't ready to give up yet. Bill cocked an eyebrow at me and said nothing. Ellen cleared her throat. When it was time to pay up I gestured to the Chumbo. He took his time arriving, also part of his charm. I had been calculating and arranging Spanish words, silently rehearsing them. As he slammed our change on the counter, I gave him what I thought was an over-the-top compliment and a full intensity, thirty-two toothed smile. It had always worked on old ladies and gangs of bikers.

Bill made a sound through his wine. Ellen was busy pretending she didn't know me. Just for a moment I thought I saw a twitch at the corner of the Chumbo's mouth, an ephemeral shadow of a smile, a certain softening of his hard expression. Then it was gone, replaced by a slight roll of the eyes in the approximate direction of heaven as he stalked away.

Bill contained himself until we got to the car. He started the motor and I saw that he had to pause to wipe his eyes.

"Okay, I give up," I said. "What did I say that's so funny?"

"You really have got to work on your Spanish, Art," he managed. "That's probably the first time anyone has ever told the Chumbo that he looks just like their mother, only better."

Aparicio was waiting for Bill when we got back to his farm, sitting on a stone wall smoking a Ducado. His horse was nibbling at the tall grass near the edge. We sat down with him and he and Bill carried on a conversation that was indecipherable except for the occasional word. My Spanish had got me in enough trouble, so I just listened, trying to let the rhythms of their speech register in my brain. From time to time Aparicio would look at me and grin. Once he laughed out loud, and I was pretty sure Bill was describing my gaffe at the *tapas* bar in Ugijar. He had such an agreeable face that it didn't bother me.

He was a slight man, but surprisingly strong. Bill told me that he had once lifted a fallen mule at the bottom of a ditch onto his feet when the owner had despaired of getting him out. He always wore a soft cloth cap, and I imagined him sleeping in it. He had one of those faces that never rests, mobile eyebrows that rose and fell in time to his words, and a way of crinkling his eyes that women have told me was flirtatious and devilish. He could work uninterruptedly for ten hours, or, on days like this one, as we drowsed in the sun, sit for just as long and with just as much enjoyment. The black tobacco cigarette lay on his bottom lip, jouncing as he spoke, wreathing his head in a halo of smoke.

After a while he took a bundle of cut stakes from the saddlebags of his horse and with Bill started pacing off the land that would become the garden. Ellen and I watched.

"Know what?" I said suddenly. "I wouldn't mind seeing this garden when it's finished."

31

Ellen said nothing, but I thought I could see her brace slightly. She did that whenever I came out with a new idea for our lives. Not resistance, just caution, like you exhibit when you are walking with an alcoholic friend past a liquor store.

"Who knows? Maybe we will," she said noncommittally.

.

Later in the day, Antonia, Aparicio's wife, turned up with two of their granddaughters. She was a strong-featured woman with muscular arms and no shyness of strangers. The girls were about ten and twelve. Both had that glossy nearly-black hair that is the legacy of their Moorish ancestry, but both also had piercing blue eyes, which I later came to know was from the Galician, and therefore Celtic, genes in these parts. At first they hung back shyly, but Antonia threw herself right in, chattering animatedly to Ellen without being concerned that she wasn't understood. She took Ellen by the arm and led her to the front of the house, where some stones had been piled in the form of a rudimentary cooking fire. By gesturing broadly, she made Ellen know that she was to collect firewood. Antonia opened a cloth bag one of the girls was carrying and started unloading containers and pots. Barking an order, she dispatched the eldest to bring water from the spring above the house. I moved away nervously, in case she had something in mind for me. But I needn't have worried: this was something that women, and only women, do. All four of the women worked, and as they did I saw Ellen merging easily into the activity. Despite her natural shyness, she even tried a few words, which made Antonia laugh. They were getting along fine.

Bill told me that they were going to cook *migas*, a traditional hearty meal of wheat and recycled stale breadcrumbs. It was a delicacy that people rarely bothered to make these days, since the preparation was arduous. This was not only for our enjoyment, as it turned out. She wanted her granddaughters to learn how to do it properly, over a fire in the countryside, the way she and her mother had done it during hard times in the past.

I helped Bill and Aparicio pace off distances and unroll string to mark the boundaries, while the fire was started and Antonia bent to her task. Every once in a while, Aparicio would stop and point to something he saw, or perhaps, envisioned. I was aware that Bill and he were seeing what was going to be, rather than what was. I could feel myself getting drawn in. Once Aparicio told me to stand in a certain spot with one arm in the air while he and Bill sighted over me from the house stoop. I realised that I had temporarily become the new pergola, and felt honoured.

A while later we heard the sound of a car motor from the road. A dusty red Mercedes pulled over and parked on the hazardous curve and a tall man in city clothes got out. Bill froze for an instant.

"Hell," he said. "It's Roberto. He must have seen us in Ugijar." He climbed onto the terrace above and went towards the drive, where Roberto was carefully descending in his unsuitable shoes. Aparicio ignored him. He handed me a couple of stakes and a hammer and made me follow him to the far end of the garden, shaking his head. Over my shoulder I could see Bill standing with hands on hips while the other man spoke, carving the air with hand gestures. He pointed in our direction and I saw that Bill was shaking his head. Roberto waved at me, and I returned the salute automatically. Bill said something else to him and Roberto laughed. Their body language was not friendly, and I wondered if there was going to be some sort of physical confrontation. Aparicio pulled my sleeve, indicating that I should drive a stake at a spot where he was pointing. It seemed to be a completely random spot, and I realised that I was being kept busy.

Bill was now standing between Roberto and us. There was no doubt that he meant to prevent Roberto from joining us. The Argentinean was still smiling. He held something aloft that looked as if it might be a business card and stuck it in the crotch of a pear tree. Still smiling, he turned and stalked up the drive to his car. Bill watched him without moving. When he drove away, spraying gravel behind him, Bill picked up the card and put it in his pocket. He returned wearing an unreadable expression. I was strangely embarrassed, as if I had somehow been responsible. Even so, I didn't mention it to Bill, and we went back to work as if nothing had happened. Only Aparicio seemed to notice that the afternoon had just darkened slightly. He cocked one mobile eyebrow and grinned like a jack-o-lantern.

An hour later we were eating *migas*. Antonia had laid out a cloth on the ground and put the puffy grains of the dish into a large communal plate. Next to this were piles of grilled sardines, raw onion and sun-dried red peppers. The seven of us sat cross-legged on the ground and dug out a section of the *migas* with a spoon, in the traditional way. You just carve out the slice of the platter in front of you, leaving little walls of the grains between you and your neighbours. These get thinner and thinner as you dig in. With your left hand you grab a pepper or a fish and alternate bites. Aparicio opened his knife and cut small slices of garlic in his palm, popping one into his mouth with each bite. He offered me one, but I declined. The granddaughters ate as heartily as the adults, and I could see that Antonia's lesson had been a success. We went through a Pepsi bottle of strong red wine. When you finish, there is nothing else to do but lean back and rest.

The sun was now behind the tallest hills to the west and there was a slight chill in the air. The cooks took the dirty pots and dishes and washed them at the edge of the terrace, one holding the water pot while another scrubbed. Ellen's face was flushed with food and effort, but I had rarely seen her look so happy. Aparicio picked his teeth with his knife and lit a cigarette. Bill stood up and brushed off his trousers and gestured for me to follow him. We went inside and he took Roberto's card and handed it to me without a word.

"What would I want with this?" I asked.

"I don't know. I just thought you might want to make up your own mind."

"I just *look* stupid," I said. I tore the card in two and then four. "Coming to a new place is always more fun when you can tell the good guys from the bad guys," I said, and saw him smile.

It was getting darker. The women left. We had said thank you in every way we could think of, but Antonia shrugged it off. They went up the drive lugging the sacks of equipment, the girls looking every bit as competent as their grandmother. We went to pile into the car, but Aparicio, mounted on his horse, signalled to me. I went over and shook his hand.

"*Te gusta?*" he asked me. When I looked puzzled he indicated the whole of the surroundings. "La Alpujarra?"

Understanding, I said, "*Si*. Absolutely, *si*."

"*Pero ahora te marchas, no?*"

I tried to explain that we had to go in the morning, gesturing in another idiot pantomime, but Aparicio just shook this off.

"*Volveras*," he said, turning his horse, one eyebrow cocked. "You'll be back."

Chapter Five

The Way to Calle Del Rio

Aparicio was right: we did come back. A year in a poor village in the mountains of the Dominican Republic near the Haitian border had passed quickly, though not without incident. Living without a source of fresh water or sanitation, fifty miles from the nearest town along rutted dirt roads, had hardened us and ultimately given us both a case of dengue fever. This is an insect-borne illness that is sometimes called "break bone fever" because that's what it feels like. Then, after a long recuperation, an automobile accident left us both in cervical collars for six weeks, and finally ended our stay.

But we had learned to get along in Spanish. They say there are two good ways to learn a foreign language. One is "*sobre la almohada*", literally, across the pillow, meaning you take a foreign lover. The second way is quicker, if more drastic: you just go and live in a place where nobody speaks anything else. You learn fast, or you don't stay.

A week after arrival in the DR, I was asked by the host organisation to give a short speech to about a hundred and fifty farmers explaining the project we were undertaking. I stayed up for two nights with my dictionary and practised on Ellen. We thought it sounded all right. To this day I am impressed by the courtesy of Dominican peasants, who sat unflinching as I began by saying, "Ladies and horses, I am very pregnant today." But time seems to work things out, and even though we frequently despaired of being able to master the language, gradually it began to make sense.

I was a little surprised that Ellen had agreed to travel the hard road back to the Alpujarras. It could have been that I kept her interested through the long year in our palm board shack. I used to lie awake and think of the coolness of the mountain slopes and the rush of clean water in the creases of the hills. We knew that we would have to go somewhere to rest and reflect, and to decide if our vagabond lifestyle could continue. By now we were inured to Third World hardships; any discomforts of the rural life of the Alpujarras would seem like luxury to us.

So on a blistering afternoon in September, Ellen and I stepped out of Latigos' taxi onto the road above Bill's little farm. The year had brought great changes. The little yellow house had grown, with a new porch and an elegant-looking outhouse. There was another one-roomed building nearby, perched on the edge of the steep slope to the river. The garden had bloomed, and sweet peas curled boisterously around the pergola.

Bill met us in the drive and we carried our bags down to the shade of the porch. We had a lot to tell, and so did Bill, but somehow we didn't do a lot of talking right away. Instead we sat with a glass of cold tea and just took in the landscape. Where we had watched Antonia make the *migas* all those months ago there was a shallow pool shaded by a plantation of bougainvilleas and a healthy looking young walnut tree. Bill had found lily pads for the pond with some difficulty, he told us, and managed to locate a few large goldfish. Then something miraculous had happened. One day he awoke to the unmistakable sound of frog courtship. In the middle of this dry environment, miles from anyplace where water might collect on the ground, frogs had materialised. This had been no surprise to Aparicio, who had a theory that frogs fell with the rain. Maybe so. It's as good an explanation as any.

The garden was lush and thick with fruit and vegetables. Next to the pond was a strawberry patch, and even though their season had passed, Bill found us a few fruits to nibble on. He was experiencing a harvest overload and had been trying to give away courgettes and runner beans without success, because everybody else in the valley had the same problem. The trees were also in fruit. Purple figs hung heavily from the trees near the path, so thickly in fact that the slippery fallen fruits made navigation on the stones treacherous. The almond trees were nearly ready for harvest, too, the furry pods turning brown in the September heat.

There was some new fauna as well. Bill had acquired, as you do, a pair of dogs, Sadi, a doe-eyed fluffy minx, and her son, Hippie, a large, curly miscreant with a permanent gleam of friendly disobedience in his eye. They had been passed from *finca* to *finca* until finally deciding that they lived with Bill. A pair of goats was tethered to long ropes at the end of the garden, clearing the ground for expansion. Bill had started milking at once, and now had extra to give to the dogs, who in this season of heat mostly lay panting and burr-covered in the shade. Bill himself was leaner and darkly tanned. He wore new calluses on his hands and a peaceful expression.

We could stay as long as we liked. He could use the help, and we needed a base from which to make decisions about where to go next. To me, there was no question. This place could be a base for times in between our work contracts in the Third World. It was perfect for this, because, as V.S. Naipaul had pointed out, Spain is "south of north and north of south." On a clear day, it was said, you could actually see the continent of Africa from the high spots, and yet, for all that the Alpujarras are a poor, rural area, you were still in Europe. Perching on this continental cusp appealed to me. As Ellen often said, I liked keeping my options open, and what better place to do it?

I realised that, however much we would love to have a small farm like Bill's, it was not a practical idea. The land is bountiful, but only to those willing to work it, and work it hard. You can't leave a farm unattended for a year at a time. It doesn't work, for one thing, and, for another, it's somehow just not right. If we made a temporary home, it would have to be in the village, capable of being locked up and left for long periods. We remembered with pleasure Bill's rented house in Latigos, and I thought we should look for something similar. We slept soundly on that until Bill shook me awake at six a.m. and asked if I wanted to help with the milking. I supposed so.

The year before, returning from Ugijar, we had passed what seemed to be a small village about a mile below Bill's farm. I asked him about it over breakfast. He said that it was called Cantilla, and that it was bigger than it looked, stretching from the road all the way to the river.

"What's it like?" I asked.

Bill shrugged. "Just an ordinary pueblo, I guess. I've only been down there a couple of times. Two bars, two shops. They've got a lot of water down there, though. A lot more than Latigos. Sometimes they get into quarrels over it in the dry season."

All I could remember about it was a few houses on a curve and an extraordinary large rock beside the walled cemetery, the size of a freight car, painted white. I looked at Ellen.

"Want to take a look?" I asked her.

"Might as well," she said.

"There's a short cut below my place, along the *asequia*. It'll save you a few minutes walk."

"No, thanks," said Ellen with a glance at me.

The closer we got to Cantilla the greener the world seemed to get. Whereas Latigos sported a lot of carefully irrigated fields, Cantilla seemed to have water everywhere. Even the weeds on the verges were tall and healthy looking, as if it had recently rained. We came around a sharp bend over a sheer drop of maybe thirty metres, with no guard rail. Someone had recently laid a bundle of flowers at the roadside, indicating that at least one unlucky vehicle had gone over. The flowers were dead and the ribbon showed tire tracks. An almond tree part way down the incline had been sheered off by something falling heavily. This was not a road people would drive unless they had to.

Another sharp curve opened onto a massive church and a row of buildings stretched along the top of the road. One house had an ancient olive tree growing through the foundations over the road. The branches were thick with small, pale green olives. Ahead we saw a sign, an arrow pointing left and announcing the direction of the *centro urbano*. We turned down a steep, paved street under the church and passed a fountain surrounded with flowers. An old man across the street stopped hoeing his garden patch and stared. We waved cheerfully and he called out a greeting. He watched as we descended through a thick cluster of houses on a street no more than eight feet wide. A woman looked at us from her *camara*, two stories up, but vanished inside when we waved. Two dogs followed us barking obsequiously and running every time we turned to look at them.

This village showed its age. Not just in the sense of needing a coat of paint, which some of it obviously did, but by its design. Clearly no one had anticipated the automobile when the streets were laid out. I had a feeling of being in a *medina*, the old section of a North African town. We stepped over an open trench running along the road, relieved to realise it was an irrigation canal rather than an open sewer.

We turned a corner and found ourselves in a plaza. Not the picture postcard type you find in tourist villages, with pretty fountain and shaded open-air cafes, but a cemented square where a few trucks were parked beneath the façade of the *ayuntamiento* , or town hall. The houses facing the plaza were tall with wrought iron balconies and shutters, now mostly closed. A cluster of old men sat on a ledge in a vanishing strip of shade against one wall. Apart from a few dogs and a mule tethered in front of a drinking fountain, there was no one else in sight.

Hesitating for just a moment, I greeted them.

"Yes, good day," they responded.

"It's hot, isn't it," I said.

"Yes, yes," came the chorus. They weren't showing a lot of curiosity. I was a little disappointed. Without looking at Ellen, I said, "We're looking for a house to buy."

This was greeted with silence. I persisted.

"We'd like to buy a house here in Cantilla," I said, ignoring a pointed nudge from Ellen. The men seemed to absorb this without comprehension. One of them resumed weaving a lasso from *esparto* grass. I stood uneasily, wondering if my Spanish had suddenly deserted me. Surely people weren't all that accustomed to strangers asking for real estate. Later I realised that this had been just too outlandish to be dealt with seriously.

We went over to the fountain and edged carefully next to the mule. I drank the cold water that ran day and night into a horse trough. I put some on my face against the steadily rising temperature in the square. When I looked up I saw one of the old men, leaning on a walking stick, standing behind me. He was wearing a sweat-damaged fedora hat and, incongruously, a cardigan sweater.

"You want to buy a house here?" he asked. His accent was thick and his speech rapid.

"Yes, if that is possible," I replied.

"Why?" he asked. I looked to see if there was any trace of irony on his face and found none. It seemed that he was genuinely puzzled, as if to say, "Why would anyone want to buy a house here?"

"We are friends of Bee," I explained. "The foreigner who lives up the hill." There was no sign of recognition from the man. "We, uh…"

"We think Cantilla is beautiful," Ellen broke in. "The most beautiful village in the Alpujarras."

The man shook his head and gave us the windscreen wiper sign. "No. Cantilla is not beautiful. It is ordinary." This sounded like oft-repeated conventional wisdom. "But," he said, allowing a smile to overtake his broad face, "It is more beautiful than Latigos. Don't you agree?"

"Of course," I lied. "That is why we have come."

"Well," said the man. "It just so happens that I have a house for sale, a very good one. I could show it to you."

"Yes, please," I said, and followed as he walked creakily down a road leading off the plaza. I saw that we had drawn a crowd. Four or five of the old guys, two children, a dog and an old woman, who squinted at us but did not respond to our greeting. The road led steeply down. There were flat stones set on edge in v-grooves in the middle, to provide traction when it was wet. We passed what seemed to be a grocery, where a sturdy-looking woman stood watching from behind a fly curtain. We drew up in front of a roofless three-storey house built on a corner astride a slope so steep that the front stairs were a yard taller at the bottom than at the top. The old man gestured with his stick.

"That's one of the finest houses in Cantilla," he said. "My father, who was a master mason, built it himself. I was born just there," he pointed to a window on the first floor. I couldn't help noticing a large diagonal crack in the front wall, large enough to put your head in. He anticipated my observation.

"A sack of cement," he said. "That's all. A day or two to dry and then you'll have a mansion."

Someone snorted behind us. It was the owner of the grocery, a thickset woman with recently permed hair. She stood with arms folded a few paces behind the crowd, which I saw was growing by the minute.

"That house was a ruin when I was born, Pepe Senior," she said. "And your father herded goats."

The old man growled. "Remedio, what does a woman know about construction? We are talking man to man here." He turned back to me with an air of mock exasperation, as if to say, "Women."

Remedio grabbed one of the taller children and whispered in his ear. He took off up the street, running.

"Why don't you come in and have something cool to drink?" she said to Ellen. "If the men want to talk foolishness, let them stay out here in the heat. I have sent for someone who will show you a proper house to buy." She led Ellen through the bead curtain. I shrugged at Pepe Senior apologetically and followed. The crowd, now at least a dozen strong, waited in the street.

Remedio took us through her small crowded shop through a door into a small bar built at the rear. It was closed for the afternoon, but she opened the doors onto a terrace with a dazzling view of village rooftops. Light streamed in. She offered us beer, but we settled on some of the alcohol-free wine. A teenaged girl wandered sleepily into the room rubbing her eyes. Remedio sharply dispatched her to mind the store.

"These people aren't used to foreigners," she said, pouring the wine and sliding a plate of peanuts as a *tapa* in front of us. "But I am from Ugijar, where we have seen many hippies such as yourselves." She didn't pause, and I didn't spill my drink. It was clear that she thought the word "hippie" was descriptive, as, say, "farmer" was; not a pejorative term.

"The people of Cantilla are very friendly, but they are not well educated. You need to deal with people of more experience."

The fly curtain parted and another woman appeared. She was tall and fine-boned, with iron-grey hair tied in a severe bun and an expression on her face which can only be described as anguish. She wore an elegant black dress and a black lace shawl, one end of which was thrown across her throat. At her side was a young woman, also in black, with thick glasses and a wandering left eye, who had the attentiveness of a courtier. She nodded to Remedio and stood with arms at her sides looking over our heads as if at some point of rescue out of our line of sight.

"It is my pleasure to introduce you to Agustina," Remedio said smoothly. "Agustina, these hippies are interested in buying your house in Calle del Rio."

Ellen made a sound that I couldn't identify, somewhere between a gasp and a guffaw. I started to speak, but found my Spanish had temporarily deserted me. Agustina still did not look in our direction, but nodded, as if receiving messages from some unknown source.

"That is why I have sent for you, Agustina," Remedio went on melodiously. "The house your dear husband built would seem just the perfect place."

Agustina turned a severe gaze in my direction. It was like looking at a player in a Greek drama. Her eyes were dark portholes opening onto a whole wide sea of suffering. She bathed me in anguish for a moment, then said, "Please follow me."

I followed obediently toward the door. Ellen nudged me. I looked back at Remedio, who was looking expectant.

"One hundred pesetas, please," she said.

The crowd was still waiting for us in the street. It had grown to include two young women with babies and a fat boy eating sunflower seeds from a bag. Agustina strode elegantly through them. The girl lieutenant lurched clumsily along behind. We straggled down two steep streets and passed along a railing overlooking an orange grove. Dogs slunk out of the way and cats scrambled up drain pipes to the roofs. We were too large a crowd to walk side by side. With the unconscious intelligence of the herd, we expanded and contracted to fit the narrow containers of the streets.

We were near the bottom of the village, heading toward a cluster of houses that projected into the fields. We turned left sharply and I had to duck as we passed through a tunnel obviously formed when somebody had decided to expand his house over the right of way. We entered a very steep, very narrow road, where the houses seemed taller overhead. At the end of the street the village ended in a stony track that led into the countryside. There were three houses on our left. We stopped at the first. It was wider than the others and had an elegantly high carved wooden door and rich mouldings in the plaster. Agustina took a key from her pocket, wrapped in a white handkerchief, the only visible article of her clothing that wasn't funereal black. With a look of great solemnity she wrenched open the bolt that had grown rusty with disuse. She pushed open the door, and I noticed that despite her ethereal appearance, she was quite strong.

Ellen and I went in. Agustina stayed in the open doorway, bracing herself against the arm of her wall-eyed lieutenant. We found ourselves in a foyer that might have suited a city house in Madrid, were it not for the dust and fallen plaster. There were doors to both sides. I pushed one open and found myself in a large sitting room at the foot of a wide staircase down which light was streaming. The proportions were grand, and if it were not for the litter of construction rubble and neglect, it would have been impressive.

"Nice and bright in here," said Ellen. She pointed up the staircase and I saw why. Above the first floor the roof was entirely missing. It didn't look as if it had fallen in. More as if it had never been finished. We walked gingerly up the stairs, which were obstructed by bricks and hardened bags of plaster. As I neared the top, a sudden rush of wings made me almost lose my footing. Bats. Hundreds of them, disturbed in their perches under a finished piece of roof, swooping in panic near my head and streaming out through the missing ceiling. Ellen gasped. I realised that I was standing in several inches of what is called guano, a useful agricultural commodity, but hardly a selling point for an estate agent. I shook off a feeling of panic and disgust and turned around. Ellen was already at the foot of the stairs, breathing hard.

Agustina was still in the doorway. If the house was less elegant than her formal aspect implied, she showed no sign of it. We later learned that she had not been inside for more than twenty years. The crowd jostled politely for position as we emerged. I was speechless, but Ellen thanked her politely for showing us her home and said we would be in touch with her as soon as we had discussed it. Agustina gave a long sigh and locked the door in the same, almost sacramental, style with which she had opened it. She nodded, and without actually looking at either of us, strode back up the street, her lieutenant behind her. Looking briefly undecided, the stragglers followed her, leaving Ellen and me alone in the street.

"How did you like it?" said a voice behind us. It was a youngish man seated on the step of a house across the street. He was holding a sleeping baby in his lap and smoking cigarettes. He wore a pair of tortoise shell glasses with a patch over one lens. He was dressed in a freshly starched white shirt and creased trousers. He was small of build and had delicate looking hands, unlike the other men we had seen in these parts.

"It was… interesting," I said.

The man slid over, gesturing for us to join him on the stoop. "Do you know why that house was never finished?" he asked with obvious pleasure. Then, without waiting for a response, he told us.

Agustina was the widow of a local master builder, called Emilio. He was born in Cantilla, but at an early age had apprenticed himself to a *maestro* in Granada, where he learned the fine techniques of masonry seen in the wealthier houses of that city. He was a tall and handsome man who had acquired elegant city manners. It had always been thought that he was a good cut above the others of his generation. When he returned to Cantilla to marry, he had brought some of the techniques of construction back with him. He found work in a few places, mostly constructing public buildings, because the ordinary people could not afford his elegant style of work. He had begun work on the house we had seen in the last year of his life. It was to have been a fine example of city architecture and a place for his family to live. He had arranged to buy the houses adjacent, rough places of no particular value, to demolish and make room for extensive gardens.

One day, about twenty years before, he had been working on the upper story of the house in the hour of dusk. He had raised a load of cement to the roof and was mixing it and applying it to the overhang when, for reasons still unknown, he fell. A neighbour woman found him lying on the stones as she returned from her garden. She raised the alarm and a mule was fetched to carry Emilio to the plaza, where he lived in a large house belonging to the family of Agustina. He was unconscious, and his limbs were twisted so that everyone was afraid to straighten him out. Someone ran to the Guardia Civil post up the hill, and in about an hour an ambulance appeared and took him and his distraught young wife to hospital in Granada.

He was in hospital for several weeks. Agustina remained by his bedside, and only sketchy information arrived in the village. One day in midsummer an ambulance arrived in the plaza and Emilio was carried upstairs to his bedroom overlooking the fountain. He was, said the women who had insinuated themselves far enough into the gathering horde to get a glimpse of him, paralysed and perhaps blind, since his staring eyes did not blink. Agustina disappeared inside and was not to be seen for many weeks.

Cantilla endured a terrible summer. There was drought, and temperatures rose to alarming levels. During the evenings the shutters of Emilio's room were opened and a torrent of sobs, curses and screams of pain went on through the night. Even the most cold-blooded of gossips tried to avoid passing under the window. Men stayed huddled at the other side of the plaza and spoke in hushed voices.

It took Emilio until September to die, which he did one midnight, amid sounds of pitiful wails and pleading, interspersed with choking noises that sickened everyone who heard them. When he had finally breathed his last, Agustina could be heard for the first time, keening in a way that stole the strength of the religious and made even teetotallers throw back an *aguardiente* in the bar. No one who was alive at the time could forget that night.

Shockingly, Emilio's funeral had taken place in Granada, with only a few family members in attendance, and he was buried quietly in the Cantilla cemetery the next morning, attended only by a priest. Agustina was not seen for several weeks, and when she finally emerged one morning before Mass, her black hair had turned the colour of iron, as it was today.

Ellen and I were silent. This was more than we needed to know about Agustina and her house. The young man seemed to enjoy the tale, though. He sat smiling, smoking cigarettes and blowing the smoke over the baby's head. He introduced himself to us as Francisco, and we shook hands with him in a subdued way.

"So, are you going to buy Agustina's house? We could use some neighbours in Calle del Rio," he said.

"Sorry, I don't think so," I said.

"Then buy mine," said Francisco.

Chapter Six

Hard Bargaining

The spare house Francisco wanted to sell was next door to Agustina's. We had been looking at it without knowing it. The front was narrow, with a peeling, bolt-studded door and one window on each of the three storeys.

"Here," he said, and handed Ellen the baby, who was sleeping as if anaesthetised. He went inside and came back with a huge old- fashioned key and pushed open the door to the sound of protesting hinges and a cloud of dust. Inside was a stone-floored entryway with a laundry sink covered in flakes of fallen whitewash from the cane ceiling. A dirty floral shower curtain hung concealing a hole in the floor covered by the lid from a can of paint. We could see that this was the sanitary arrangement for the residence. At the back of the entryway was another heavy wooden door that stood half-open. Francisco pointed and said,

"Corral. For the pig and the horse."

He led us up a flight of stairs that were built in a surprisingly elegant curve to a narrow room overlooking the street. Opening the shutters, he revealed a cracked cement floor and flaking walls painted a noxious yellow. The room was perhaps sixteen feet long. At the rear was a partition wall made of plastered cane with a door no more than five feet high. We went through this into what we realised was a large room divided into a warren of smaller ones, plainly bedrooms for a large family. At the back of this, a good twenty feet away, a window opened onto a view of an empty field and the river.

Francisco seemed unconcerned by the parlous state of the property. He smoked and made comments about the spaces as we entered them with no trace of self-consciousness. He led us up a second stairway to what had plainly been the family kitchen, consisting of a low hearth, a rickety table, and two broken chairs. Opening the shutters revealed a view over the roof of the houses opposite to the lush *vega* beside the river. Behind the kitchen there was a door made of patched scraps of plywood that led us into the *camara*, or storeroom attic. This was a large room with a sixteen-foot ceiling and a stairway made of pegged olive wood that passed through a hatch onto the roof.

The *camara* was like an artist's studio, streaming with north light from the high window that etched interesting shadows on the bare stone walls. The artist in Ellen was clearly struck by this. She stood in the centre of the room and turned slowly around, still holding Francisco's baby. She had been rolling her eyes as we passed through the squalor of the downstairs; now I could see that something had touched her imagination. I followed Francisco onto the roof.

Estate agents recommend that you put out fresh flowers and boil a pot of coffee if you want to show your house to prospective buyers. You don't lead them through a warren of dark rooms without a flushing toilet that needs plaster and paint. But if you know that at the end, on a rooftop in the Alpujarran sky, there is a view so breathtaking that it beggars description, you might be able to afford Francisco's casualness.

Behind the house the Sierra led upward to the village of Bayarcal, perched in the seam of the mountain, and on beyond that to slopes covered in pine and *encina* oak until they vanished into clouds. In front ran the river along winding flatlands punctuated with eroded red cliffs and planted in rows of maize, barley and fruit trees. To one side the edge of the valley rose through terraces of olives and then the sere branches of almonds and figs. To the other, Cantilla climbed the hill with white houses topped by washing lines until it reached the spire of the church. Up on the hill, the cemetery could been seen, with its rows of cypress trees and the enormous white rock behind.

Ellen came onto the roof, and I took the baby from her arms. I must have thought that the sight might loosen her grip. She stood blinking as I had done in the sunlight. Francisco was chattering away, as if oblivious to this vista he had seen every day of his life. I wanted him to shut up for a moment, so that I could record this sight. I handed him the baby. A light breeze came from the direction of the river. It was filled with an unlikely perfume composed of freshly cut grass, citrus fruits and aged horse manure. Sheep baahed their flat calls to each other, and somewhere, out of sight, we could hear the brassy tones of a woman singing *cante hondo* to no one but herself as she slapped clothes on the washboards of the fountain.

Ellen and I tried not to look at each other. We followed Francisco down through the maze of rooms to the street. He sat on his stoop and explained that the house, though basically sound, might need a bit of work. "A sack or two of cement," he said.

Still not looking at Ellen, I asked how much he was thinking of asking for the property if we were interested. He didn't answer, but invited us upstairs to his kitchen, which faced the first floor of the house, and we sat at a table by the window. He brought out a Pepsi bottle half full of local wine, some bread and the remains of a cured ham. We drank politely and he drank thirstily. The ham was wonderful. He explained that the meat had come from his own pig, and that it had lived in the corral of the house we had just seen.

Francisco was a poet. It took him all of ten minutes to begin reciting couplets he had composed. He brought out a dog-eared copy of a magazine published for a local centenary celebration, in which he had rhymed the names of all the local villages and spelled out something of their character. As the wine disappeared, we heard how he had tried to study to be a priest until he had failed an unfair and illogical exam. His accent altered, became more formal, with lots of rolled r's and husky j's. His gestures became broad, almost theatrical. He held the baby in his lap and fed him from a bottle as he told us that this was his second son, who would also be a poet. The baby showed no signs of his father's vocal traits. He just drank milk and slept again. I remarked that they didn't make babies like that where I was from.

It was getting late. He said that soon his wife would return from working in the commercial greenhouses of the coast. We should stay and meet her. She would cook dinner and we could go to the bar and buy more wine. He would borrow a guitar from a friend, and we could have a party. We would make good neighbours.

We begged off. The wine was clearly getting to Francisco, and we wanted to see some more of the village while there was enough light. At the door, I asked him again about the price of his house, if we were interested. He waved his hand dismissively.

"We'll discuss all that tomorrow," he said.

We walked up to the plaza by a different route, a small road that clung to the edge of a stone terrace wall above an orange grove. We were still not looking at each other.

"You don't just buy the first place you see," Ellen said, as if to herself.

"Nope."

"And you don't stick yourself with huge renovation bills and all that hassle."

"Definitely not."

"The roof was actually missing in a few places. It had been raining in the *camara*. You could see streaks in the whitewash."

"Really."

We reached the top of the village and looked down from an *era*, a stone circle built on a rise formally used for winnowing wheat. Men were returning to the streets from the fields, pulling their mules and horses, which were laden with piles of wood, maize stalks and boxes of vegetables. Some boys, released from school, were taking turns kicking a football against the wall of the church. There were a few more cars in the plaza, and we could see the fly curtain of the bar swinging as people went in for their afternoon wine and *tapas*.

"How much do you think he wants?" Ellen asked.

Bill was amused. Yes, he knew Francisco. A good man who liked a drink and didn't work very much. He had something wrong with his eye, some kind of accident. His wife Mari supported the family. Three kids. When he got drunk he tried to play the guitar, but he couldn't do anything but strum. Couldn't even tune it. Sang. Not a bad fellow, all things considered.

"How much is a house like that worth?" I asked. We were just finishing a dinner of fried eggs, fresh bread and string beans from the garden, washed down with spring water.

"How much do you want to pay? It's kind of a buyers market, as you can imagine."

"Needs a hell of a lot of work."

"That room with all the partitions must be twenty feet square," Ellen said. "And the attic. You could put a pool table in there."

"Now there's an idea," I said.

"I mean it's large."

"Yes, it is."

We washed up, still talking about the house. Bill listened with a knowing smile on his face.

"Would you come down tomorrow with us?" I asked him. "I could use a little help with translation, and I'd like to know what you think."

"Sure," said Bill. "But I don't think it matters much what I think. You two have already bought it."

Francisco was at home when we got there. So were his brother, Jose, and his wife, Mari. She was an energetic woman with blonde hair escaping from beneath a headscarf and eyes that darted constantly around the room. Jose looked like an older version of Francisco without the delicate hands. We sat in the dilapidated kitchen of the house we were going to buy on a collection of broken wooden chairs. Bill sat draped over the staircase, looking at details of broken plaster and rotting beams. At one point he had jabbed his pocket knife into a ceiling beam and watched it disappear easily. Jose smiled and shook his head, saying that the outsides had been eaten by worms but not the centres. He struck the beam and shouted, as if we were nearly out of earshot, "Strong. Strong." I looked at Ellen, feeling a small shiver of panic, but she just shrugged.

Francisco was enjoying himself. Like all true poets, he had a disdain for mere business. He conducted things as if this were a seminar he had organised.

"Well, neighbours," he winked with his good eye. I looked again. I had been sure that yesterday the patch had been on the other. "We are pleased that you like our little home. We would never have left it except that we keep growing as a family, and we need more room."

Mari leaped in, looking at Ellen, and began a speech, between women, about the difficulties of raising a family. Ellen nodded sympathetically.

"I guess we'd better hear what price you're asking," I said, feeling that I was being culturally insensitive, but wanting to head off worse embarrassment later.

"This is no cheap little place," Jose said, gesturing with his callused hands as if he were holding a plough. "No, sir."

"It has been a good home," Mari chimed in. "A loved home."

I nodded sympathetically. It was clear that there had been much discussion since yesterday.

"Nevertheless…" I said, looking at Francisco meaningfully.

"Well," he said, "After having thought long and hard, and after consulting with my family, I will have to say that we wouldn't be able to entertain an offer of less than two hundred and fifty thousand pesetas."

I did some rapid maths and concluded that he must have made a mistake. That was just about fifteen hundred dollars at that time. It was much less than we had assumed. I half expected Jose to jump in, but he just looked toward me resolutely.

"*How much?*" asked Ellen suddenly.

"All right, then," said Francisco quickly. "Two hundred thousand, and that's my bottom offer."

"No," said Ellen. The room went silent. I sighed. I had been expecting this. Bill raised his eyebrows and looked at me. I was about to speak when Ellen went on.

"That's not enough. We'll pay two-thirty-five and not a *centavo* less."

A look of consternation scrambled Francisco's features. "How much?" he asked, looking at Jose, who was bobbing his head urgently.

"Two thirty-five," I said. "Last offer."

"We'll have to take this under advisement," Francisco began, but Mari ignored him. She grabbed Ellen's hand.

"Done," she said.

Two days in the Alpujarras, and we had bought a house.

Chapter Seven

Cats and Frogs

I awoke before light and sat bolt upright in bed. I had been dreaming about roaming through an enormous house with hundreds of windowless rooms, all of which were ankle deep in guano and threatening to fall down. I got up and went out onto Bill's stoop and watched the sky turn pink behind the mountains to the east.

Had we really bought a house in Cantilla? I felt the shape of the huge key in my pocket and wondered if we had briefly lost our minds. I was astonished that Ellen had seemed so enthusiastic. That was usually my department. Last night we had sat up with Bill and discussed legal matters, the ins and outs of construction, and swapped ideas for the new shape of the house. We retold the story of the purchase over and over, laughing as we remembered Francisco's face when Mari had said, "Done!" I hatched plans for a heat-re-circulating fireplace. Ellen caught my mood. She talked about hand-glazed tiles for the new shower room. What we hadn't done was think through what it would mean to live in a place we hardly knew, among people we hadn't even met.

Just before we left Botswana, after two years spent fruitlessly trying to unravel the problems of rural poverty, my friend Jonathan asked what we were going to do next. I reeled off a list of possibilities. Most of them involved finding someplace where the living was easy and the property cheap. Ellen listened stoically. When it started to sound unrealistic even to my ears, I trailed off. Jonathan, wise beyond his thirty years, said, "You know, Art, there are no little undiscovered fishing villages left. They've all been found and turned into tourist traps." I nodded, but thought to myself, "We'll see." It was clear Jonathan had never been to the Alpujarras.

I left a note on the kitchen table and left Ellen and Bill to sleep the sleep of the innocent. Stepping carefully, I made my way to the road, followed by the two dogs. Once on the pavement I was able to see well enough to navigate. The dogs turned around at the first curve, realising that I wasn't likely to provide any breakfast.

Cantilla was still asleep when I reached the church. Walking carefully through the streets I managed not to disturb anyone except one old dog who barked half-heartedly. The plaza was deserted, though I realised that several of the vans that had been parked there the night before had left, carrying men to work in the greenhouses near the coast.

The house looked unfamiliar to me in the gloom of the pre-dawn street. I turned the key in the lock and groped my way to the sink, where Francisco had told us the ceramic fuse holder was kept. It fitted into the bare electrical box. A light went on upstairs and lit my way up. A twenty-five watt bulb hanging by a wire from the ceiling made the room look even grimmer in its dim glow. I put my hand on the flaking yellow wall and felt plaster falling away. There was a smell of disuse and damp. I couldn't reconcile what I was seeing with the enthusiasm of last night. I went upstairs to the *camara*. As I stepped onto the landing I saw patches of light where the brightening sky shone through the holes in the roof. Opening the shutters, I found myself looking into Francisco's kitchen across the street. There was no one about. Mari would have gone by now in one of the vans to work in the fruit packing houses of El Ejido. I sat on one of the ruined chairs and tried to imagine myself into home ownership.

There was a sudden crash from the room we had already begun to call the studio. Startled, I leapt to my feet and knocked over the chair. Yanking open the door, I saw that a glass jar containing dried-up olives had fallen from a ledge under the door to the roof, which had been left ajar. I went in carefully, letting my eyes adjust to the dimness. Midway into the room, I had one of those instinctive tingles of the neck that we have inherited from when our ancestors had more hair. I wasn't alone in the room. I couldn't hear or see anything, but I was certain of that. I stopped dead in my tracks, listening to the sound of my own breathing. Nothing moved. It's a rat, I thought. Just great. I had never considered vermin in my plans for the house.

I started for the stairs, intending to open the hatch and let in more light. Something rushed past me. I could hear claws scrabbling on the floor and instinctively jumped aside. An animal, larger than any rat of my experience, raced through the doorway. I swore, more out of fear than anger. I spun and saw a cat the size of a cocker spaniel perched on the window sill. It had a grey muzzle and a look of murder in its eyes. I had the impression of one chewed-off ear and a tail bent in the middle. It hissed and jumped through the window and was gone. In its wake was malevolence as palpable as a smell. I shook myself. A cat. Maybe a big, evil cat, but a cat nonetheless.

"What was *that*?" Bill's voice came from the stairway. He and Ellen were halfway up, holding a flashlight.

"Nothing," I said. "Just a cat."

The house by daylight seemed more promising. They had brought a thermos of coffee with them, and we sat on the roof and watched the sun come up. Dawn was slower in this river valley because of the mountain range to the east. Even after it was light enough to see, the sun was held behind a ridge until, with a sudden dazzling burst, it lit up the tops of the hills to the west. People were moving around in the *vegas* below with horses and mules. Francisco turned on his radio and waved at us through his kitchen window.

Bill kicked at the surface of the roof, dislodging dried grass that had sprung up from the clay surface. He exposed a layer of rotten plastic sheeting and some broken canes below. Bouncing with one foot on one of the poles that served as rafters, he diagnosed a whole new structure for the roof patio side of the house. This was narrow, only about eight feet or so. It wouldn't be expensive, he said, just a hassle to get the materials and haul them up to the roof. You couldn't actually buy these materials, he explained. When the house had been built, poles were cut and carried from poplar groves along the river, peeled and cemented into place. On top of these were bundles of *cana*, a bamboo-like cane that grew in ravines on rough ground. The plastic was no problem. Then we would have to get someone to haul us a good many loads of *launa*, the grey clay that went on top. That was several days work for a man with two mules, he said.

This sounded unlikely at best. Couldn't we substitute some other materials, I wanted to know.

"The best thing to do is hire a mason to do the whole thing," Bill said. "You and I can do the inside work, but you need someone with access to pack animals to bring sand down here. There's no way to get a truck within a hundred yards of the house."

"Where will we find a mason," I asked dubiously.

Bill grunted. "One will turn up."

As Ellen pointed out later, the arrival of Guisado was just like the arrival of the frogs in Bill's pond. Bill had gone home. We were wrenching partitions away from walls on the first floor, choking in clouds of dust, when a head popped above the staircase.

"*Bueno dia*," said Guisado. He invited himself in, a stocky figure in a white painter's cap and overalls, carrying a canvas tool bag. Later I realised that he had come all ready to start work. My approval was assumed before we had even met.

"*Buenos dias*," I said.

Guisado introduced himself. "I am Antonio, the master builder. I see that you need my help."

"Could be," I said cautiously. "A little renovation work is needed, that's all."

He sniggered unpleasantly. "You need a new roof, complete re-plastering, plumbing and partition walls built, am I right?"

"Well, I guess that's probably about right."

"Let's get started then," said Guisado.

Guisado was not his real name. His mother had called him Antonio, as his wife and the priest did now. Everybody else called him *guisado*, which means "stew pot." His *apodo*, or nickname, was never used to his face. This was true of nearly everybody in the village, where of perhaps a hundred and fifty adult males in Cantilla, at least half were named Pepe, Paco or Antonio.

Later that year I would be waiting along with everybody else in the village outside the plaza bar for the arrival of the man who collected electric payments for the utility company, La Sevillana. The man would arrive with a stack of bills in envelopes and begin calling out names:

"Jose Rodriguez Alcantara! Francisco Velez Rubio! Juan Martinez Velasco!" and nobody would answer. A few women would huddle, and say, "Oh, yes, that's Pepe El Grillo ("Joe the cricket") or Paco La Oreja ("Big-eared Frank"), which was how they had been known since childhood. Even though everyone would know what his nickname was, they would never hear it to their faces, when it was always Juan or Paco or Pepe. Not everyone's *apodo* was in itself embarrassing. My friend Paco the taxi driver was known as just that, Paco Taxista. But in many cases the nickname revealed something shameful or laughable about one's character.

Antonio had been known as Guisado before he left the village to spend some years as a bricklayer in Madrid, which experience had made him put on a few airs which didn't endear him to the villagers. Somebody must have given him the name at some time in the past, for reasons unknown. Over the time we worked together it would come to make perfect sense to me.

We showed Guisado what needed doing. Most important was the roof. He dug into the *launa* and rotten cane with a sneer.

"You should tear all this off and put in cement beams and ceiling," he said. "Cover it with tiles. This is the old-fashioned way of doing things."

"Call me old-fashioned," I said.

He began to tick off what we would need. Ten poplar beams, eight bags of cement, a load of sand, three loads of *launa*, and then something I didn't understand, called "machimbrow."

"What's that?" I asked.

He put a finger through a circle of thumb and forefinger and made obscene motions, sniggering.

"What?"

"Look," he said, holding up his finger. "*Macho*." Male. He held up the circle of forefinger and thumb. "*Hembrado*." Female. I realised he was talking about some sort of tongue and grooved roof tile called *macho y hembrado*, which had been mangled by his Alpujarran accent.

"And *telafatica*," he said. "Six rolls."

"Let me guess," I said, "Asphalted cloth. *Tela asfaltica*. Tar paper."

"And a gas cylinder for my burner," he said.

Guisado didn't write anything down. I asked him if he wanted to make a list. He shook his head and tapped it with his finger, indicating that it was all in there. It was only later that I discovered that he could not read.

"Where do we get all this stuff?"

"The sand comes from the river." He pointed downstream. "The poplar logs from the corral of my father-in-law's house. You are lucky he has a few to spare. Everything else they will bring from Ugijar."

We went downstairs to look at the toilet drain. We would need a plumber, he said. He could make the bathroom walls but could not do the pipes. Unfortunately the plumber was the Communist candidate for mayor, he told us deprecatingly, but his work was all right even so. Guisado made another unwritten list of bricks, mortar and plaster. His head must have been filling up. He was getting happier by the minute, and my doubts were growing. I looked at Ellen, who was not quite rolling her eyes.

"What do you think?" I asked quietly.

She shrugged. "Looks like it's too late now," she said.

Between Cantilla and Latigos lies a fault line. Everything on the Latigos side that goes wrong is the fault of Cantilla, and vice versa. Only two miles apart, they had a completely separate history, vocabulary, even accent.

Cantilla had existed since the time of the Moors. A few years previously, some archaeology students from the university in Granada had spent several weeks digging in a field belonging to the church. They had found a Moorish cemetery and the remains of a mosque dating back to the eleventh century. Latigos, by contrast, had been built during the reign of the Catholic kings after the expulsion of the Moors in the sixteenth century, which gave Cantilla a five-hundred year head start. Latigos was settled by immigrants brought to the valley by the Catholic invaders from places like Galicia. That is why you see children there with blue eyes and fair hair. As a term of abuse, Cantilleros referred to people from Latigos as "Gallegos," and even "*forasteros,*" or outsiders. A mere four hundred years wasn't enough to make them locals.

Because of their long history, the Cantilleros had pre-existing rights to most of the water when Latigos was founded. Although Latigos had much more farmland, and a greater population, it was stretched out over the breast of a mountain, instead of hugging a moist valley as Cantilla did. In the long dry summers the struggle for water would reach drastic proportions, sometimes leading to midnight forays by farmers from Latigos to divert trickles of Cantilla's water from the high mountain streams onto their own land. There had been several cases of violence when this happened.

Cantilleros, on the other hand, had to put up with the indignity of having Latigos established as the local seat of government. The town hall for the valley was located there, as was the doctor's surgery. The *Guardia Civil* post was built at the entrance to Latigos because of its strategic position at the foot of the mountain highway.

People from Latigos spoke scornfully of the Cantilleros, calling them dirty, uncultured and dishonest. When I had been there about a year, the Sunday supplement of the Granada newspaper published an article about the amazing number of children to be found in the village. This was true. While other local places of the same size had to share schools, having a children's population of a few dozen, Cantilla had its own school and an infantile population of over a hundred. With tongue in cheek, the paper had speculated that this might be because of something in the water. Within days, lines of cars from places as far away as Jaen were furtively arriving in the plaza and filling jerry cans of water from the fountain, to be given to the unhappy childless of the province. At first, Cantilleros were proud of the mention in the paper, until subsequent articles quoted people from Latigos saying that their neighbours had all those children because they never went to work, but just stayed in bed all day doing what comes naturally. Cantilleros were enraged, and several leading citizens denounced the statements from Latigos. The traffic for the water slowed, but never dried up. Even today it is possible to see some hopeful prospective parent skulking near the fountain with water containers.

It is not unusual for two neighbouring pueblos to have this animosity. I have seen it in other parts of the world as well. Gerald Brennan discusses the phenomenon as it existed in the twenties between nearby Yegen and Valor, in his book, *South from Granada*. But I have to say that I believe the bad blood between these two places tops it all. Three kilometres in the Alpujarras is a million miles.

Which is why Aparicio was scowling when I spoke to him that afternoon back at Bill's. He was chopping maize stalks with a sickle and I was helping him to bundle them up and load them onto his horse. He kept shaking his head every time there was a mention of our new house, traitorously located in Cantilla. He asked me why we had done such a thing.

"Well, Aparicio, we didn't know there was any problem. It's a good house in a pretty location, that's all we knew."

"My brother-in-law's house is for sale," he said. "I could have got you a good price."

"Well, maybe we were a little hasty. Still, it's done now, and I'm happy."

"You know not to drink the water," he said. "You know that's why there are so many people with crossed eyes down there."

"I hadn't heard that, no."

"Carry your drinking water from here, from Bee's spring," he said darkly. "You can't be too careful around those people."

"That's an idea," I said. I looked at Bill for help, but he was examining something with great concentration on the other side of the valley.

"You can't trust any of them. No one."

"We have to trust somebody, though. Or else we won't get along. Today we hired a mason, for example."

Aparicio's ears twitched like his horse's. "Who?"

"His name's Antonio."

"Antonio? What Antonio?"

"Stocky guy. Used to live in Madrid. Strong, but laughs like a girl."

"Guisado!" Aparicio bellowed. "Bee, you couldn't have let them hire *Guisado!*"

Bill just shrugged, but when Aparicio's back was turned, he gave me a wink.

Chapter Eight

A Sack of Cement

At eight the next morning Guisado arrived with his *peon*, a cadaverous man of sixty with a hacking cough and a bitter expression. He was leading two magnificent black mules. Guisado called me down from the kitchen, saying we had to go to the *rambla* to get sand. Ellen and I were just beginning to make progress tearing down partition walls. She seemed as involved with the project as I was. I didn't see why I was needed at the *rambla*. I said so.

"This one, Jose," said Guisado, jerking his thumb at the older man who now sat smoking on Francisco's stoop, "he can't work very hard." He gave me a significant look, *"Rinones."* *Rinones*, or kidneys, as I was later to learn, were cited as the cause of every back pain, of which in this rough country, there were many. I was about to ask why he had been chosen for the work, when I realised: these were his mules. I looked at him puffing black tobacco and coughing convulsively every few seconds and realised that my wall-clearing project would have to wait.

We set off down the track at the end of the street, Guisado leading, Jose holding the reins and me lagging as far behind as I thought prudent. I'd had to deal with horses and mules a number of times in Africa and Latin America, but I still thought it was an activity best left to rich people on weekends. I had been one of a small group in the Dominican Republic trapped in a railed enclosure when a stallion *"se puso bravo,"* as the locals said. We would say, "went insane." Dodging a furious thousand-pound beast while trying to remain upright in six inches of manure hadn't endeared me to the equestrian experience. I had been the last one over the fence, and, thereafter, the last one to go near the stallion. So I lagged back out of kicking distance, even though these mules seemed docile enough. Guisado kept calling for me to keep up as we reached the river and crossed at a wide narrow ford. I got water to the knees of my jeans missing slippery stepping stones, but kept a look of stoic unconcern on my face.

The *rambla* was a canyon cut into the opposite bank of the river. It rose gradually above us to a branch of the *asequia*. When water was plentiful, the river washed across the bank, gradually, over many years, leaving a bed of sand and gravel behind. We unloaded a pair of screens nailed to wooden frames, which would be used to filter the sand from the gravel. Guisado handed me a flat shovel and we began. Jose held the horses. I shovelled. Guisado shook the frames over a sheet of plastic. Gradually a small pile of grey sand began to appear.

Every so often Guisado would bundle up the plastic and dump the sand into the big woven baskets on the mules.

The sun got higher. I was beginning to sweat. My hands had lost some of their toughness since I had left the Dominican Republic, and nascent blisters appeared. I puffed. Guisado kept up a continual torrent of chatter consisting of obscene jokes and anecdotes demonstrating his manhood, strength and wiliness in the tough streets of Madrid. Jose coughed rhythmically and said nothing. He had not uttered a word since he arrived. The saddle baskets were filling very slowly. When one mule was fully loaded, I handed Guisado the shovel. He began shovelling at twice the rate I had, looking pointedly at me and urging me to shift the screens faster. Finally both mules were loaded. I straightened up with difficulty.

"Okay, Arturo," said Guisado. "You go back with Jose and unload the sand in front of your door. I'll wait here and get some more sifted."

"Why don't you go back and unload it?" I replied. "And I'll wait here." I wasn't even sure how to get the sand from the saddle baskets without getting uncomfortably near the mules. Anyway, who was the boss here?

"Okay. You go next time, then."

"Wait a minute. How many loads are we going to need, anyway?"

"At least fifteen," said Guisado. "Maybe twenty." I did a rough calculation. This load had taken an hour and a half. Twenty loads would take thirty hours, three and a half days.

"Can't you buy sand around here?" I asked, trying to keep the panic out of my voice.

"Sure," said Guisado, "but this sand is free."

That was my first introduction to Guisado economics. That afternoon I bought a truckload of sand from Ugijar.

Here's how you carry an eighty-pound sack of cement from the plaza down to the bottom of the village:

Get someone to put it on his mule. If no mules are available, being needed to haul sand, get someone to put it on your back. Lean forward, bend your knees slightly and put both hands at the base of your spine to support the bottom of the sack. If there is no one to put it on your back, use the following method. Pick up the sack like you would a baby, as casually as possible, as there are people watching to see just how strong a foreign man might be. Sling it over your shoulder in one casual motion, at the same time leaning forward, to allow the sack to slide down your back. If it hasn't slid neatly down your back, raise and lower yourself on your heels sharply, maintaining a look of indifference. When you have the sack in place, set out down the sloping street, past the clutch of pensioners hugging the shade of buildings, avoiding, if possible, fresh piles of horse dung, as these may be slippery. Ignore the children running in circles around you, calling out "Hey-lo!" the English greeting taught in the first year of school. Avoid contact with large four-legged animals tethered across the narrow street. Also avoid contact with Guisado, who has a snide comment for almost every occasion. Blow the sweat off your eyebrows without using too much valuable breath. If your legs are trembling, wait for a suitable moment and lean against a building out of sight of the neighbours. Keep going. When you reach the house, shed the bag with as much nonchalance as possible and act with forbearance as the peon's sardonic laughter turns into a liquid tubercular cough. Accept the glass of water from a concerned spouse, who wants to remind you that nobody is too young to have a heart attack. Don't raise beseeching eyes to heaven and ask why you thought a house on the bottom street of the village was such a good idea.

Next time you are in Ugijar, buy a wheelbarrow.

After no more than a week all the materials were in place, and Guisado and his *peon* Jose were up on the roof. Alongside our mountain of sand, cement and bricks, another pile of detritus grew steadily as Ellen and I ripped out old walls and chipped away at loose plaster. We now had one large, loft-like room on the first floor about forty feet long, narrow on the street side, but widening out towards the back into a generous L-shape.

Defying local custom, we had decided to make the first floor into a kitchen at the narrow end, meaning that it would be the first room you entered when you came up from the foyer-cum-corral. The room was blessed with unusually high ceilings, so that our kitchen would be higher than it was wide. Behind this we planned a big lounge with my dream fireplace and a bedroom tucked out of sight around the corner.

We were a little disheartened to see that the floor was coming up in chunks where we removed partition walls. I dug through and found that the original poor-quality cement had been poured directly onto the canes that sat on the floor beams. The floor would have to be removed and re-poured, or else some ingenious local solution would have to be employed.

I asked Guisado. He said that we could pour new cement directly on top of the old. All we needed to do was put in some metal mesh to bind it together. That would make the floor very thick, and awesomely heavy. I wondered if the old beams below could take the weight. Guisado shrugged. "Try it and see," he said.

Another discovery gave me pause. While the front and rear walls of the building were made with stones two feet thick, the side walls seemed to have been built with compressed soil and small stones. This meant that where age and dampness had made the plaster fall away, there was no firm surface behind on which to spread new plaster. We hammered and chipped away at the surface, which had been covered so many times with whitewash that it was nothing more than a fragile skin. It came away in plate-sized pieces and left ugly brown holes behind which I despaired of trying to cover. Bill suggested anchoring metal screens to the wall by pounding long nails deep into the compressed earth. This seemed to work, but was very time-consuming. After two days, I had managed to cover an area of wall no bigger than a large dining table. Guisado came down with a bucket of cement and began trowelling it on the mesh. Then he snorted and began slinging it at arm's length directly into the holes. It stuck. That was good news and bad news. The good news was that we could repair the walls without completely excavating them. The bad news was that this meant a lot more of Guisado, and more time before we could move in.

The roof was almost finished. The top surface was covered with thin bricks whose edges sat inside each other ("machimbrow"). This in turn had a layer of tar paper seamlessly stuck together at the edges by a gas torch. On top went the first layers of *launa*. The rest of the roof, the largest section over the "studio," was stripped, covered with tar paper and then buried under *launa*. It was an attractive roof from the top, with new, weed-free silvery clay much better than our neighbours. From below, though, in the narrow bit of the top floor we had decided would be a second bedroom, the raw bricks atop the new poplar beams looked out of character. These would have to be plastered, Guisado told us delightedly. If he was going to keep finding new work to do, Ellen pointed out cynically, we might as well let him move in with us.

At the back of the large new lounge we found an area of wall that had previously been connected with some sort of interior structure. Guisado told us it had been a traditional beehive oven, one in which fire was built and let to burn hot, ashes and coals banked, and the dough added once the heat was sufficient and left until baked. He joked with Jose that we were not only hippies and foreigners, but also "*panaderos*." Jose just scowled.

Later I asked Aparicio why being a baker was so funny. He explained that *panadero*, or baker, had been a term of contempt for people who worked a ruse during the *hambre*, or years of hunger following the Second World War. Because the Allies blockaded Spain to chastise Franco for his assistance to Hitler, the years around 1945 were ones of terrible famine. War had disrupted agriculture and imports were halted. People in Cantilla and Latigos were reduced to eating figs, which they hate to this day, and even boiling river grass. In an effort to alleviate the situation, the government had provided quotas of flour and grain to each village. The wheat was sent to those families who were bakers.

A few unscrupulous individuals, including, it seemed, the former owners of our house, had built ovens and declared themselves to be bakers. In reality they kept most of the wheat for themselves, a con that made the situation much worse for the village. After things were back to normal, a kind of subsistence poverty the right side of desperation, the term *panadero* was extended to include any form of collaboration with the landlords, government or any other oppressors.

"Guisado should know," Aparicio said, spitting, "His family were some of the worst *panaderos* in the village."

We chipped out the stones marking the oven and plastered over it in the end. A wardrobe now covers the evidence.

Chapter Nine

An Honorary Man

When you're doing construction there are a million little things you need. In a city there's no problem running out to a hardware store to buy nails, silicone putty, sandpaper and rubber gloves, but when you're in a remote place like Cantilla, purchases become an effort. We had been asking Bill to get us things on those occasions when he had to drive to Ugijar. He hadn't complained, but I was beginning to feel guilty. Sooner or later, we would have to buy our own car.

Cars were thin on the ground in Cantilla. The recent relative prosperity of the village brought about by the expansion of the huge greenhouses on the coast and the work they provided had begun to make a difference, but as yet just a few people had vehicles. When people had to travel, they relied on the so-called pirate taxis.

Every village had at least one taxi. Ours was driven by Paco, a paunchy, round-faced, handsome fellow with a bandit's moustache. He had recently returned to Cantilla after ten years away, working in Barcelona and the Canary Islands. For this reason he had a more cosmopolitan world view than his contemporaries did. He and his wife, Consuelo, had moved into a house beside the plaza that had been his childhood home. Consuelo was a pretty, shy woman that was rarely seen among the others at the shops. She spoke in a low murmur, making the listener lean forward to catch her words. Paco clearly adored her, often bringing her gifts from Granada when he returned with his carload of passengers. He had foregone the big money he had been making working outside the village in order to raise a family, as he said, "In the real world," meaning the rural world of Cantilla.

Paco drove a load of passengers to Granada in his Peugeot 504 every morning of the week except Sundays. To ride with Paco, you had to go to his house the day before and pull the rope that hung from the first floor, which was connected to a bell that summoned Consuelo from her chores inside or in the garden. She would write your name down on a list and tell you in a near whisper to be in the plaza the following morning at 5:15. When I went for the first time, she wrote, "hippies," because she was too shy to ask my name.

Ellen and I made a massive list of things we needed from the big city, even though we knew that as soon as we returned there would be something else that we hadn't anticipated. There were such things as pots and pans, although both village shops had a small selection. There was cloth for curtains, throw rugs for the tile floors, a shower curtain in the event that the shower was ever finished, and mattresses and cushions for the bed I was going to build us in the first floor bedroom. The list was far too long to complete in one go, we knew, but we could make a start. Some of it we could carry on our laps, and some of it would fit on the roof rack of the taxi. Anyway, though neither of us would have admitted it, we were longing for a restaurant meal and the sights of city life.

There was no way that we would be able to get to the plaza at that hour from Bill's house, so we decided to spend the night in the house for the first time. It was well roofed now, and even though full of construction materials and rubble, we would be able to clear a space on the floor for our sleeping bags. We had a few functioning electric lights and running water. It was already better that some of the places where we had been living in Africa, so why not?

At the end of the day we washed ourselves and changed out of our work clothes and went for the first time to the Plaza Bar. This was a converted corral in a fine house in the plaza. It opened twice a day, once at five a.m. in order to serve the workers their shots of brandy and black coffee with which they started their day, closing about eight o'clock. Then again at nightfall, when the same workers would return from their jobs and begin an evening of drinks and *tapas*. The bar had been taken over recently by another Paco, the son of the owner, and his wife, Paqui. They were in their thirties, contemporaries and good friends of Paco Taxista.

When we got there the place was filling up. Men were standing belly to the bar in what seemed to be a chaotic scrum. The cement floor was littered with used paper napkins, cigarette ends and leftover bits of food that were being fought over by three small dogs with undershot jaws. It was like making an entrance in the saloon in a Western movie. The bead curtain parted, and conversation came to an abrupt halt. As in the Latigos bar the year before, no one stared at us, but we felt like something on a laboratory slide. We went through to the back room, where there were a couple of tables. As we sat down Paco switched on the lights and a bare bulb shone on us like a spotlight. I hadn't noticed, but Ellen was acutely aware that, apart from Paqui, she was the only woman in the place.

Paqui, perhaps because of her profession, wore her face in a severe expression that I only occasionally saw change. She looked at us for a moment. I was hearing a non-existent drum roll. Then she nodded, not at me, but at Ellen, and, as if by magic, conversation resumed. We later learned that women never came into the bar except on special occasions, such as during the *fiesta*. What seemed at the time to be a forbidding encounter was in fact an acknowledgement of a new state of affairs that women from an earlier generation would have found hard to accept. Without knowing it, Ellen and I had started a new rule: foreign women, poor uncultured things from far away, would henceforth be treated as honorary men. Paco, probably also unaware that history had just been made, asked us what we would like to drink.

The institution of the *tapa*, which literally means, "lid," is an integral part of Spanish life. It fills a gap in the gustatory day essential to the schedule of life. The workers who left Cantilla each morning would begin at dawn with a shot of brandy or a mixture of anise and brandy called a *sol y sombra*, taken with coffee and perhaps a sugary roll called a *bollo*. That would serve them until about eleven in the morning, when the first break of the day happened, when they would eat a *bocadillo*, or sandwich, prepared by their wives the night before. Some stalwarts drank a beer or two with this. Lunch was at three o'clock, and was usually taken in some nearby cafeteria. This was a meal of two or three courses, almost always featuring a *caldo* (hot soup) or *guisado* (stew). At least a half bottle of red wine would accompany this. It was in the evening that the *tapa* came into use, tiding over hungry men until their evening meal at ten o'clock.

The Plaza Bar served beer in bottles and red wine made in a local village and poured from a wooden cask. This was as strong as undistilled fluids could be made, something on the order of thirteen per cent. Its colour was slightly yellower than most red wine, the characteristic of the hardy Contraviesa grape. It would not make wine connoisseurs fill newspaper columns with praise, but, as a friend of mine says, you get used to it, because the bottom half of the bottle tastes better than the top.

Every time a beer or glass of wine is served in rural Granada, a *tapa* is given free. These vary according to the contents of the owners' larder. In the case of the Plaza bar, most of the vegetables came from Paqui's own garden. On a typical evening, you would see four or five *tapas* served in sequence, so that everyone had a variety. There would be *berengena frita* (fried battered aubergines), *calamaritos* (deep fried young squid), *longaniza* (locally made sausage), *pollo al ajillo* (chicken wings grilled with garlic, and *habas con beicon* (small broad beans with bacon). Sometimes, if the owner had been fishing or hunting, there would be trout fillets or pheasant. The portions were generous enough so that three or four *tapas* would take care of the dinner needs of the average foreigner, and the red wine ensured a good night's sleep.

We gorged that night on *chorizo*, stuffed eggs and sardines. Ellen stayed with the alcohol-free wine, but I drank the stuff from the keg. It was beginning to taste better the farther down the barrel we went, and I might have gone on sampling it if Ellen had not insisted. I pushed my way through the crowd to pay the bill, but Paco shook his head and pointed down the bar at a cluster of men near the door. The bill had been paid, I gathered, by the man in the bandit's moustache.

"Who is he?" I asked Paco.

"The *taxista*," Paco answered.

Ellen and I went past Paco Taxista on our way out. I offered my hand, and he took it in a beefy grip he had got from years of using machetes in the cane fields of the Canaries.

"Arturo," I said. "We just bought a house here."

He smiled politely "So I hear."

"I guess word gets around pretty quickly."

"You might say that."

"Well, thanks for the drinks."

He waved a hand as if shooing flies. "See you at five-fifteen."

When we reached the door he called after us, "Watch out for that *panadero*."

We had forgotten the alarm clock. I lay on the floor gliding in and out of dreams, afraid to miss four-thirty, when we had decided we needed to get up. The hangover helped. The wine had left my mouth so dry that it stuck together. Every once in a while I glanced at the luminous dial of my wristwatch and agreed with myself to take a brief nap. By three-thirty I was too stiff from the hard floor to stand it any longer. Groping my way down, I went to the laundry sink in the foyer and drank a quart or so of water. The darkness was almost palpable. There was no sound except the distant rush of river water. Leaving Ellen to her sleep, I went carefully upstairs and climbed onto the roof.

It was chilly in the pre-dawn air. I let my eyes accustom themselves to the dark. Gradually I could make out the shape of Bayarcal and its few streetlights to the north. Just one or two lamps indicated where Latigos was half concealed by the shoulder of the mountain. Cantilla's lights were clustered near the plaza. I saw one insomniac's light shining from the window of a house two streets above. Further up the hill a dog barked perfunctorily. I was alone in a world I hadn't known existed until a few weeks ago, but I felt myself beginning to relax into it, as you do with a bath. I was standing on my own brand new roof, sturdy and firm beneath my feet. I was tired from lack of sleep and mildly poisoned from the red wine, but I felt fine.

My watch said four-fifteen. Time to begin to rouse Ellen. I put a foot on the ladder down to the studio and pulled the hatch behind me. I was halfway down when I felt something grab my trouser leg and scramble up my back. Letting go, I fell backwards onto the floor of the studio, while a cat, the same wild, rangy cat I had seen the first morning, leapt through the gap in the hatch and, with a harsh, primal howl, disappeared. I lay on my back and tested my joints. Nothing was broken except my mood.

Ellen said I should forget about the cat. I was beginning to obsess.

"Poor thing was probably more terrified than you were. Maybe it was hunting mice. It could be a good thing."

"Is there such a thing as a cat trap?"

"Don't be ridiculous. Just leave out a bowl of milk and make friends with it."

"What about poison?"

Ellen sighed. "That's immoral. Probably against the law, too. Stop making such an issue of it, and watch where you climb in the dark from now on."

I rubbed my backside. "It's me or him," I muttered.

Chapter Ten

Why There Are No Gypsies in Cantilla

The trip to Granada takes two-and-a-half hours if you are lucky. When the pass at La Ragua is closed after landslides or heavy snows, it is necessary to take a different route, and the journey can last double that. We headed north and uphill in the dark, getting the jump on any traffic and giving ourselves a good chance of arriving in the city by eight o'clock.

I sat up front with Paco and Ellen wedged herself between a large woman with a streaming cold and a nervous old man who clutched his walking stick tightly between his knees. The jump seat at the back held two children and their mother. She held three plastic bags that Paco had issued her in case of carsickness. Not everyone in Cantilla had gotten entirely used to car travel, especially when travelling the hairpin bends of the mountain highway. I was a little nervous myself, if for no other reason than remembering the trip up here over a year ago.

Paco chatted to me as he drove. He had had more experience of the world than most. He was able to imagine being in such places as Botswana and Santo Domingo. We traded stories. He corrected my Spanish without shyness when I made a mistake. He was a philosophical man who listened to debates on Spanish national radio while driving the roads. He was not shy about his opinions, which ranged from the surprisingly liberal (women's employment rights) to the scarily right wing (forced deportation of illegal aliens). His conversation was peppered with anecdotes and the occasional dirty joke, told in a respectfully low voice which Ellen, even though straining forward, could not quite make out. Sometimes I laughed too hard and had to shoot her an apologetic look over my shoulder.

Bits of fallen rock littered the roadway in the mornings before the highway workers had had time to clear them. Paco was casual about these, sometimes slowing to a crawl to negotiate a patch of rubble, other times swinging close to the edge where there were no guard rails. As we left the pass and headed down, there was a sheer drop of several thousand feet on an outside curve. I was involuntarily gripping the seat when Paco suddenly said, "Arturo, look!" He was holding both hands clear of the wheel, waggling his fingers like a magician in the middle of a trick. He was steering with his knee, which I couldn't see in the darkness, and I would have derived little comfort from it if I could. According to people I talked to later, Paco often did this stunt, but only if he liked you.

Granada was a-crawl with traffic by the time we arrived, and a thick layer of smog was visible during our descent from the mountain road. We caught just a glimpse of the Alhambra palace before diving into a melee of squealing brakes and car horns. Our destination was a square at the centre of the traffic, where all the pirate taxis had their base during the day. With admirable unconcern Paco found a place to park the taxi near the cathedral, and we piled out stiffly. He pointed in the direction of the Plaza de la Trinidad and told us to be at the Bar Soria no later than four o'clock.

It's easy to get distracted in Granada. There is a famous line about it that has a beggar saying to a passing woman, "Madam, take pity on me, for there is no fate worse than to be blind in Granada." We had hours in which to take it all in, the staggering sight of the Alhambra looming over a sheer cliff above a river, the maze of streets of the Albaicin, or old quarter, and the caves where gypsies had lived for centuries. We wandered rubbernecking like any tourists through the city. I had to remind myself that we were now residents of the province of Granada, that a piece of all this history now belonged to us. Perhaps it was because I was so dazed by the sights that I abandoned the most basic rule of all travellers: keep your hand on your wallet.

We were wandering through the narrow streets near the cathedral when three women wearing bright floral dresses and heavy makeup approached us carrying carnations. They chattered and moved like a small flock of birds, while I said, "No, thank you." One of them pinned a carnation to Ellen's collar with such speed and dexterity that she had no time to protest. I reached stoically into a pocket for some loose change and pulled at Ellen's arm. Someone jostled me and I lurched against her. I put a few pesetas in one of the women's hand, and she made elaborate gestures of pleasure. Someone spoke, and I turned to see a man in the smock of a market trader pointing at my legs.

"*Monedero*," he said. "*Su monedero*." With a sickening premonition I patted my jeans pocket and found it empty. My wallet had gone and so had the three women.

I was more embarrassed than angry at first. The man shook his head sadly and went back into his stall. I went through the motions of looking in other pockets while Ellen watched helplessly. I had been carrying most of the cash we had brought to do our shopping. She had the passports and other documents in her bag, which she had kept safe by clutching it with white knuckles during the assault of the women. I had lost money, a driving licence and, worse, a paper with a list of vital telephone numbers of friends all over the world. We sat on a bench and took some deep breaths.

"So what do we do now?" Ellen wanted to know. "The police?"

"I don't think that's going to be any use," I said. "This probably happens all the time." I examined her for any trace of recrimination, but found that she looked as shocked as I did.

We sat in a cafeteria trying not to let the incident deflate us too badly. I realised that it had been my unwillingness to offend people of a different culture that had made us vulnerable. Our years in Africa and Latin America had made us sensitive to the cultural realities of other peoples, and, in this case, too sensitive. I should have shrugged the women off, as I would have at home.

We counted the bits of money we had left and found that we could at least afford a good lunch and pay Paco our taxi fare. I would report the missing licence by mail and order a replacement. The phone numbers we could replace by a little digging. We were unhurt, if not unscarred by the experience. When we went out, Granada was still dazzling.

At the corner of the cathedral three women were approaching tourists with carnations. I couldn't be sure they were the same ones, but as I passed, one of them caught my eye. She whispered something to her companions and signalled for me to come closer.

"Did the *senor* lose something?" she asked with what was either guilelessness or the street genius of a psychopath.

"I think you know I did," I said, unsure whether to yell for the police or just ignore her.

"Look over there," she said, pointing to something lying under a public wastebasket attached to a post. It was my wallet, looking flatter but none the worse for wear. Inside were my driving licence and the little pad of phone numbers, but no cash.

"You have to be careful here," the woman said, not quite ironically. "There are thieves everywhere." She smiled and pinned a carnation to my shirt.

Paco was philosophical on the drive home. "At least you learned something about gypsies," he said. "You see, a gypsy is not a criminal."

"How do you figure?"

"The gypsies are people who have had to live among enemies throughout their whole history," he said. "Like the Jews, they were surrounded by people who they couldn't rely on, and who didn't like them. But, unlike the Jews, they stayed underground. You will never see a gypsy living in a big house or wearing fancy clothes. They tend to dress in poor clothes when they can be seen. But they have wealth. If you had shaken one of those women you would have found that she was heavier than she looked, because of the gold they sew into their clothes."

"I didn't even know they were gypsies," I replied.

"Take my word for it, Arturo. You got stung by an old gypsy trick. Tell me, do you want to go to the police?"

"No."

"Why not?"

"Because it would be useless. Besides, the woman was helping me get my wallet back. I couldn't very well turn her in."

"Exactly. A good gypsy will always sting you, but make you realise that it could have been worse. You might even feel grateful."

"Hardly." I growled. "Just not ready to cause problems."

"Gypsies don't consider us to be people, did you know that? They are raised to think that we are like fish swimming in the sea. They are fishermen. They have a strong code of ethics, believe it or not. Their women dress sexy, wink at you, make you think they are loose creatures. But they're not. You can never lay your hands on a gypsy woman, but they use our instincts against us, our own greed and lust." He laughed. "Of course that wouldn't apply to us, would it, Arturo?" winking at Ellen in the rear view mirror.

"So do they live in caravans, or what?" I asked.

"Not here. The gypsies around here live in villages and towns, just like everybody else, but they keep to themselves. They even have their own way of speaking Spanish that we can't understand."

"I haven't noticed any in Cantilla."

Paco looked at me and nodded. "And you won't. Do you want to know why?"

"Why?"

"Do you know that ruin on your street? The one below your house?"

I had noticed that at the bottom of the street there was a house with only one wall standing beside a pile of rubble. I had assumed that it was the result of many years of neglect, but Paco explained that it had been occupied until about twenty years ago. The house had belonged to a man who had since died, but now it belonged to no one.

A young woman relative of the owner had been orphaned as a teenager. She remained in her own village, to the east of the Alpujarras until one day when she contacted the family and told them she had recently been married and wished to come and stay in Cantilla. As they had an empty house, they invited her to stay as long as she wished. Though they thought it strange that they had not heard of the wedding before this, they assumed that it was due to outlandish customs of people from that end of the valley.

One day the girl arrived with the man she said was her husband. He was tall and sported long sideburns and spoke with an accent. He wore leather trousers and had a gold watch on a chain, which he often took out in the bar. They moved into the house, which had recently been repainted and furnished with donations from the curious neighbours. The relatives had signed over the deed as a late wedding present.

The couple weren't seen much by the villagers. The girl spent some days with her relatives, but never talked about her husband. If the family thought this was strange, they didn't say so. The girl was shy and plainly innocent, and she had been dealt a hard blow with the loss of her parents. The husband never visited, and it was unclear how he made a living. He had a large truck, which he parked on the outskirts of town, and sometimes he would be away for three or four days together. No one hesitated, except in the presence of the family, to say he was a gypsy.

On a chilly afternoon in November, three gypsy horse traders came to Cantilla. They drove large horse vans with trailers behind and herded their animals into the plaza, as was the custom. During the evening they bargained, sold and traded with the villagers, who, even knowing the tricks gypsies employed to make animals look more valuable than they really were, entered into transactions with gusto. Everybody thinks they can outsmart a gypsy.

At the close of the session the animals were loaded, and the three men vanished into the house of the young girl and her husband. Voices were heard through the night, voices singing, laughing and, then, shouting. Just before dawn the girl arrived at her relatives' house, wet and shivering from the dew she had collected while hiding from her husband and his friends. She was crusty with dried blood. Sobbing, she told them that, after drinking a lot of whisky, her husband had begun to quarrel with her. His friends were laughing. He picked up a hammer and struck her with the handle six times, yelling that if she didn't leave he would hit her with the heavy end. At first too ashamed to run to her relatives, she had caught a glimpse of herself in the glass of her window and seen that she was covered with blood. Afraid she might die, she had finally gone for help.

By the time her uncle arrived, the men had gone. Their trucks had disappeared from the plaza, and her husband's was nowhere to be found. By eight o'clock all of Cantilla knew what had happened. Abandoning the day's work, they converged on the house carrying hammers and picks. Grim-faced, they tore it down. It took all day. By evening the house was as it is today, nothing but a ruin.

"What happened to her husband?" I asked Paco. By now everyone in the car was listening and nodding agreement as he spoke.

"He came back the following day," said Paco. "A few people met him on the road." He paused. "That's all I can tell you," he said darkly. "But that's why there are no gypsies in Cantilla."

We got back about sundown. Paco dropped us off in the plaza. A herd of people surrounded the taxi. They waited while Paco unloaded the items he had brought back for them: two pairs of shoes, a window shade called a *persiana*, cough medicine. Paco, like all rural taxi drivers, ran errands for

Cantilleros in the city. He did this uncomplainingly, and free of charge. The villagers seemed to expect this, as if he were the postman.

Guisado and his peon had finished for the day. The lounge had now been plastered with cement. It looked enormous in the glow of the bare light bulb. We sat in the centre of the room, ignoring the smell of fresh cement and ate the goodies we had brought back from Granada: tinned mussels, fresh pate and a loaf of whole wheat bread, washed down with a bottle of white wine, something unknown in Cantilla. We decided it was too dark to walk all the way back to Bill's farm that night. We could stay at our house another night. And so, without being aware of it, we had moved in.

I lay awake for a while, thinking about Paco's story of the gypsies. Images of the people I had begun to know demolishing a house in a single day, throwing stones and beams into the river, burning canes and furniture, flashed through my mind. Francisco, with his ready alcoholic smile, Paco Taxista winking in philosophical irony, little Gregorio, the neighbour at the top of the street with his impenetrable accent, serious-faced Paco Junior from the Plaza Bar. There was a lot more to these people and this village than I had expected. I began to wonder if, by buying a house, I was doing something more than a mere real estate transaction. Something made me wonder if we were not joining something, something ancient, mysterious and not at all what it seemed.

Chapter Eleven

Other Undesirables

The weather was beginning to change. The summer sky, at times almost white with heat, had yielded to deep blue with periods of cloud that seemed to promise rain. I found Gregorio waiting on his stoop with his horse. He was a tiny man, bent from arthritis so that he always seemed to be peering at you sidelong. He had some land he wanted to sell me. Ever since we had come to the pueblo, everybody seemed to want to sell me some land.

Gregorio had officially retired. That is, at the age of sixty-five he had started receiving his small state pension and had stopped drawing unemployment benefits, which was about the same in terms of value. Since the left of centre political party had been in office, these small farmers of the Alpujarras could *cobrar*, or get unemployment payments. This had made a great difference to the local economy, and was why there had been a recent sprouting of television antennas on the rooftops and a few new cars in the plaza.

Gregorio told me what everyone else had told me, that Cantilla used to be a place of plentiful rainfall, but that in recent years there had been a drought that appeared to be permanent. He told me stories of crossing the pass at La Ragua in his youth, when there was so much snow on the ground that they had to dig as they travelled. The *nacimientos*, or springs that fed the irrigation canals still poured, but Gregorio remembered when the water shot out of the ground as if from a fire hose. The eastern Alpujarras bordering on Almeria, were in fact drying up. Bill told me that the UN had declared this area the most in danger in all of Europe of becoming desert. Gregorio didn't know much about the UN, but he spoke in the same dreary tones about the rainfall as everyone else did.

When clouds formed around the mountaintops, people went around all day glancing at the sky. But it was unlucky to suggest that it might rain, rather like whistling in a theatre. If you did chance to say that it looked like rain, a chorus of voices would rise in denial. "It never rains here," they would say, daring the gods. If it did begin to rain, people would make a point of sitting and walking about in the shower, shaking their heads and denigrating the amount that was falling.

Only sometimes, it really did rain. The river would swell to bank bursting volume, sweeping away temporary horse bridges and carrying trees downstream. Roads would temporarily wash away, and mudslides would isolate the village for several days. When this happened, the villagers would say that, yes, that had been a substantial rainfall, but that it was bad for crops because it washed away the almond blossoms or the newly fruiting olives. Or else, that this was the wrong kind of rain, that it would quickly run off without soaking the soil. Cantilleros are unpleasable. I made the mistake of speculating about the clouds overhead to Gregorio, and received the stock response. It would not rain today, he assured me. He laughed when I suggested taking a poncho, just in case.

We walked to the river, leading his horse, and climbed a path through olive groves on the other side. The land he wanted to show me never ran out of water, he said, because there was a year-round spring just above it, shared with one other farmer. To get there you had to follow what he called a road, but I would think of as a kind of shared illusion that wove between fields and terraces. Sometimes it followed the *asequia* for a while, then veered sharply upward on a stony creek bed where the horse had to be assisted. The climb was steep enough to make me wheeze a bit, and Gregorio teased me about my age and poor level of fitness. We reached a place where the olive trees gave way to groves of almonds. This was the top limit of the *asequia*: below us all was green; above us was the *secano*, or dry land, suited only for almonds and figs.

We crossed a *barranco* on a cement section of the *asequia* and started up a deep sandy track through a plantation of sisal cactuses, some of which had sent thigh-thick trunks over our heads. Gregorio's land lay in the curve of a small arroyo, where vegetation grew thickly and there was a small stand of olive trees. I followed him into a thicket of brambles to what seemed to be a swimming pool tucked under the trees. It was a *balsa*, a reservoir that collected water from the spring, which I could see thinly trickling into the other end of the pool.

There were five terraces, three of which had their stonework more or less intact. Two old apple trees, left unpruned from the winter before, were nevertheless fruiting heavily. The olives were swelling on the branches. Three rows of potatoes and a few of maize were the only planted crops. Gregorio explained that he didn't have much time to work the land, and that his son, Eduardo, had moved with his family to El Ejido to work in the greenhouses.

From the land we had a panoramic view of Cantilla and the mountain slopes above it. The huge white rock of the cemetery stood starkly against the profile of the hill. Below us was the river valley, spreading and contracting its way through cliffs to the south. People working on the land were like the ant-like figures glimpsed from airplane windows. A thin curl of smoke rose from the *vega* where someone was burning crop waste. From my vantage point I could see that a lot of the stone walls on the other side of the valley had crumbled, and in some cases, terraces had collapsed, tumbling a few trees.

I asked Gregorio if they would be repaired.

He shrugged. "The young ones are all busy," he said. "And us old ones, well, we're too old."

"That's a shame."

"Maybe you can do it," he grinned toothlessly. "Bring a bunch of hippies from where you're from, and start fixing up the land."

Ellen and I had discussed maybe buying a small piece of land to use as a garden, but this place was too big and too far away. Looking at the plot, I saw that Gregorio needed to sell because he just couldn't work it any more. Land needs attention every day, or it sours and begins to fail. I kicked at a stone in one of the terrace walls and it wobbled. A few good rainfalls and it, too, would collapse. Gregorio had known I wouldn't be interested, so he wouldn't be upset.

Just then I felt a fat drop on my cheek. The clouds I was being told to ignore were disgorging their moisture on the valley. It began to pour. We slipped and slid down the trail. The river was swelling but the bridge we had crossed was still intact. Gregorio didn't mention the rain, even when we found ourselves ankle deep in mud at the bottom of the village. I knew better than to gloat.

Francisco was on his doorstep when I lurched soddenly onto Calle del Rio. The rain had died down, but not before drenching me and covering my shoes with fresh mud. Ellen sat in the kitchen window with a mug of something hot in her hand.

"Get wet?" Francisco said. He was wearing his eye patch on the left today, though I was willing to swear that it had been on the right the night before.

"Have a look," I said, pulling off my shoes and pouring streams of water from them. "I guess you can stop complaining about it not raining now."

"No," said Francisco, wagging his finger wiper-style. "This isn't good rain. It was over too quickly. Anyway, it's bad for the olives."

In Remedio's store you have a choice of several oil paint tones for your shutters and front door: green, blue and brown. When it comes to wall paint, you have a choice of white, or white. We chose white.

The studio was nearly finished. The cement floor was good enough for our purposes, so it didn't need tiling. At the highest part of the room, the ceilings rose to sixteen feet, which meant that I had to paint from a ladder we had cobbled together from old poplar rafters. As the room turned white, it grew. It was a huge room that would be hard to find in any place where space is at a premium. Looking at the softness of the light through the hatch on the pristine white walls, even I wished I were an artist.

I checked to see whether Guisado's roofing job had held against the shower. Everything was dry except just at the bottom of the hatch, where the water level had briefly overwhelmed the little lip at the bottom. That could be easily extended for heavier rains when they came.

We began to paint the second bedroom, which had ceilings of an ordinary height and which lay under the part of the roof we thought of as the terrace. We had the portable radio tuned to one of the few stations whose signal penetrated the mountains and were listening to a combination of Spanish pop music and Bob Dylan's Greatest Hits. Francisco whistled from the street below, slapping his hand against the door that was too heavy to rap with knuckles. I looked down to see him next to a panting boy who had brought a message from the plaza.

"Arturo, there's somebody asking for you in the plaza. An *extranjero*," Francisco said. I stopped to wash my hands and went into the street. The boy who had delivered the message, swelled with the importance of his mission, started leading me up the street, as if I couldn't find the plaza on my own. Ellen raised her eyebrows quizzically.

"Beats me," I said, and started the climb.

There is almost no way to arrive in the plaza from our house with any sense of decorum. It's just too hard a climb. I once calculated that it was the equivalent of walking up to the twelfth floor of a building, except in most buildings you didn't have to dodge the fly-switching tails of tethered mules and avoid fresh piles of manure. Lately I had taken to stopping just at the bottom of the last long *cuesta*, or incline, and letting my breathing slow before making my appearance in the heart of Cantilla society. This time the boy, insensible to my cardiovascular needs, kept going, and so I arrived sweating and breathless in the square.

I saw at once who the visitor was. A mud-streaked red Mercedes was parked directly in front of the plaza bar. The passenger side door was open and a long pair of legs ending in Kashmiri boots stuck out. Music from a cassette recorder and billows of cigarette smoke issued from the car. Roberto, the

Argentinean real estate shark, leaned casually on the bonnet. He had on an unseasonable leather jacket and western boots. A small but discreet clutch of old men and children watched from the other side of the plaza.

"Hey," called Roberto, as if we were old friends, "What's happening, man?" He extended his hand, and I automatically took it, then stood embarrassed as he made a series of complicated gestures ending with us touching fists. The girl in the car put her head out the door, gave me a quick searching glance, then withdrew. She had poodle hair and makeup you need a palette knife to put on.

"You're Arturo, right?"

"I was this morning," I said, grappling for advantage in the cool sweepstakes.

"You know me, right? Roberto, right? I met you last year with whatisname, Bill, whatever."

"I remember," I said, ignoring the fact that we had never been closer than fifty yards before.

"I hear you, like, bought a house here, that right?"

"Yes."

"So, like, what's it like in Cantilla?" he spoke English in a thick Latin accent that annoyed me, because it was no better than my Spanish. He sounded like an escapee from a Cheech and Chong movie.

"As you see," I replied casually.

"Yeah, well, did you, like, run across any interesting places for sale? I'm considering extending my business up this way."

My heart sank, even though I had already guessed what was behind the visit. I was glad we were speaking English, because I knew some of the assembled audience of villagers would leap at the prospect of selling Roberto a house.

"To be honest, Roberto, we played hell finding anything good here. These people are hard as nails, really."

"Yeah?" He squinted at me and flicked at a fly with a large but soft-looking hand.

"I'm pretty sure we got screwed, too. We're thinking about packing it in and going back to Formentera."

"That right?" I thought he looked a little suspicious. "What sort of bread did you pay, if you don't mind me asking."

It worries me that sometimes I'm such a good liar. "We finally got the guy down to a million five, but I think I could have got it for a million and a quarter. The whole roof has to be replaced, too."

Roberto brought out a Marlboro and lit it ostentatiously with a gold Zippo. "You should have talked to me first. I could have got it for a million. I know these people."

"Now I wish I had. They're unfriendly, too. My wife doesn't like to go out by herself. It's not working out."

"That's too bad. Real sorry to hear it." He moved to the driver's door. "Well, get in touch if anything righteous comes up."

"Yes. Well, look here, Roberto, you don't want to take it off our hands, do you? I could make you a deal on it. We'll need the money if we move."

"Not right now, but, tell you what, I'll keep it in mind. Be cool, now," he said, staring the motor. "Ciao." The girl folded her legs back inside. They left the plaza a fraction faster than was safe.

I went home amazed by what I had just done. Not just the fact that I had done such a lot of lying, but that I had felt so strongly about protecting Cantilla from him. It was clear that I didn't want that fossil from the sixties messing up my village. Jonathan's ominous pronouncement about there being no more hidden paradises be damned. It was my village, by God, my secret. I didn't want anybody else to know.

Francisco had his baby son on his lap when I got there. He wanted to know what the foreigner wanted. I had been around long enough to know that anything you say at four o'clock is the property of everyone in Cantilla by five.

"I don't know him," I said, without remorse. "Looks like a drug dealer to me."

Chapter Twelve

Mushroom Clouds

There comes a day when you know without doubt that autumn
has arrived in the Alpujarras. It could be the mist that lingers in
the low *vegas* by the river, or the sprinkling of yellow among
the leaves of the poplars in the hills. It may be that the absence
of a sound that had become a permanent feature of your
world—the drone of cicadas—has left a somnolent quiet
behind. In this quiet you can hear logs being split with a sharp
crack in the little fields around your house. Or it may be that
when you get up you leave the blanket on your shoulders for
your trip downstairs to the bathroom.

On the day that Ellen and I awoke to autumn, Guisado disappeared.

The house was coming together wonderfully. We had painted the first floor, except for the kitchen, where a plumber, still to be found, was to install a sink and water heater. I had talked Bill into carrying some pine planks from Ugijar on top of his little car, and had built a serviceable bed. This we topped with foam mattresses that Paco Taxista had bought for us in Granada. There remained one glaring omission—my marvellous fireplace to fill the large corner of the living room. I had been ready for weeks with plans and drawings. I had gotten hold of a few firebricks from Bill. The cement and bricks and the sand for the heat-storage compartments were all ready. And I had Guisado's solemn oath that we would begin that morning.

By ten o'clock it was clear that he wasn't coming. Grumbling, I went to his house near the entrance to Cantilla and hollered up at the second-storey window. His wife's head emerged. I asked after Guisado, and she shook her head, mumbling something I couldn't understand. I thought she looked a little sheepish.

I found Paco Junior, the owner of the Plaza Bar, unloading his van in the plaza.

"You haven't seen, uh, Antonio the mason, have you?" I asked.

"Guisado?"

"Yes, that's right."

Paco smiled. "Find Bombona and you'll find him," he said. I didn't understand.

"Bombona?"

"*Setas*," said Paco, as if this explained everything. "*Setas*."

Bombona was a dapper man in his seventies who had never married. He lived with his sister Dolores in a large house near the church. He was a keen flower gardener and the front of his house, even at this season, was alive with blooms. I knocked on his door, but no one answered. Turning to leave, I saw Dolores returning home with an armful of packages from the shop. I greeted her. She answered shyly, being one of those people who still hadn't gotten her head around the idea of foreigners in the village.

"Have you seen your brother this morning?" I asked.

"No. I won't see him today," she said. "*Setas*."

"I'm really looking for, uh, Antonio. Guisado," I said, when she looked puzzled.

"You won't find him, either," she said. "It's the *setas*."

Ellen didn't know what *setas* was, either. I thought it might be some sort of annual event, like a holiday. We got out the big dictionary and learned that *seta* is a "large, flat edible mushroom, considered a delicacy." This was puzzling. I knocked on Francisco's door. He popped his head out of the window.

"Francisco, where are the *setas* around here?"

"If I only knew, I'd be getting them myself," he said.

"Is it possible Guisado is out gathering mushrooms today?"

"You can bank on it. But he's not alone. He's following behind Bombona. He's the only one who knows where to get them." I had an image of Guisado, slinking like Gollem through the forest, dodging behind trees to avoid Bombona's sight. It turns out that I wasn't far wrong.

Aparicio was at Bill's house, helping to spread fresh straw in the goat house. I told him what I had found out, and he laughed.

"That devil is just watching Bombona. The *setas* need another couple of days, so they're just finding where to come back for them. What Guisado will do, if he can, is get up in the middle of the night and take a flashlight into the woods by the river. He'll harvest all the *setas*, and when Bombona gets there there won't be anything left. He does it every year."

"Why does Bombona keep trying, then?"

"Because sometimes Bombona beats him to it. Also, Bombona knows that Guisado is slinking along behind him in the woods, so he'll make it as hard as possible for him. Sometimes Bombona wins, sometimes Guisado."

"Are they the only ones who get *setas*, then?"

Aparicio chuckled. "Once in a while someone else gets there first. Want to see?"

Down by the river below Bill's house there was little sunshine. There was a deep ravine, sheer on one side and shaded by a canopy of mountain ash, lotus and poplar trees. Even in summer a little moss grew on stones and the dark sides of tree trunks. We walked slowly along the river, clambering over stones when necessary. Aparicio stopped every once in a while and pointed to the base of poplars, where clumps of mushrooms were sprouting. They were prolific, but, as Aparicio told us, still not ready for picking. They would grow rapidly now that the weather was changing.

"Look here," he said, and with his thumb indicated a small cut in the bark of a tall poplar. "That's Bombona's mark from last year. Looks like they haven't been here yet. For some reason, *setas* don't grow in the same place every year, and a tree that's been harvested usually doesn't have any the next year. Now let me show you something else."

We climbed the bank until we reached a clearing where an olive tree, fruitless, stood abandoned. Aparicio pointed to the base of the tree, which was sprouting mushrooms.

"What's that?" he asked.

"Looks like *setas*," Bill said.

"Some people other than you have thought so, too," he said, "Only they can't tell you about it on account of they're dead."

The mushrooms looked to my eyes exactly like *setas*. Aparicio broke one off and held it up. "A real mushroom expert can see right away that this isn't a *seta*," he said, "And that all mushrooms growing at the foot of olive trees are poisonous. But there are always a few fools around." He tossed the mushroom away and brushed off his hands.

He told us a story that, like so many local tales, might just have been true. A family of Latigos had bought a sack of what they thought were *setas* from an unscrupulous trader at a street market. The woman prepared a big stew and invited her relatives over for dinner. As they were sitting waiting at the table, a cat jostled the pot and a dollop of the stew splashed onto the floor. Before the woman could prevent it, the cat gobbled a mouthful and made to jump through the window to escape.

"It died in mid-air," said Aparicio with a grim smile. "And when it landed it sounded like a piece of wood. When they picked up the cat, it couldn't be bent, it was so stiff and dead." He paused to light a cigarette.

"They had the cat stuffed, and every year they get the priest to sprinkle holy water on it, because it saved their lives."

"Groan," said Bill, but Aparicio swore it was true. He said if we didn't believe it, we could ask Mrs. Fulano when we saw her next.

Ellen looked up the word *fulano* later that night. It means "so-and-so."

The moral? Pick your own *setas*.

Guisado was back the next day, looking a bit down in the mouth. I asked him what had happened the day before.

"*Rinones*," he growled. "I had the *rinones* something terrible."

We started work on the fireplace. He didn't like the idea. People in the Alpujarras didn't use fireplaces for heat, just for cooking. These were very basic things—just a hole in the wall with a hood at head level and a simple chimney. People kept warm by using the *mesa camilla*, a round table with a pan of hot coals and ashes called a *bracero* underneath. You sat at the table and wrapped a quilted tablecloth around you, so that, even if you could see your own breath in the chill night air, your legs were warm. Some people thought this gave you varicose veins. It relied upon having a draughty house, too, because carbon monoxide build up could be fatal. Some had bought gas or electric models, and some people also used portable butane heaters, but so far at least, the fireplace as a source of heat was unknown.

I had built a few fireplaces before. I knew that the problem with most of them was that the heat went up the chimney, so the trick was to keep the heat re-circulating for a while in a chamber above the firebox. I showed Guisado the drawings I had made, but he just grunted. I decided to be patient, and we began at the beginning, making a brick hearth and sides, which we lined with fire bricks. It went slowly, with me literally pointing to where each brick should go. The back of the firebox needed to slant forward, to reflect heat back into the room. Guisado followed my orders with a sarcastic smirk on his face.

The project had become a matter of male pride. Ellen tried interrupting us with a tea break, but we shrugged her off. Guisado was in a hurry to finish, in order to show me that the fireplace would smoke and wouldn't work. I wanted to show him how superior engineering could overcome conventional wisdom. We had the smoke chamber built by lunchtime. We both wolfed down *bocadillos* and kept at it. The chimney reached the ceiling, and then joined with the chimney Guisado had already built in the studio. By the end of the day, the fireplace was finished. It needed to dry out overnight.

"You'd better wait until I'm here to light it," Guisado said. "And have a bucket of water handy to put out the fire."

"In your dreams," I said.

That night I put some ornamental tiles we had been saving in a plaster of Paris mixture and stuck them artfully to the mantle. I put a quick coat of paint on the fireplace and got kindling and a few choice olive logs from the corral. Bored with the project, Ellen fell asleep. I sat up late, anticipating the moment of ignition.

Guisado turned up late the next morning. I could tell by his red eyes and unshaven face that he hadn't slept. I realised that last night must have been D-day for the *seta* collection, and that he had been out all night trying to beat Bombona to the harvest. He didn't look happy. He complained that I had put the tiles on crooked, but I ignored him. It was time to try out the fireplace. I laid the fire scientifically, bits of paper on the bottom, followed by *mata,* fat brushwood from the dry lands, a few choice pieces of pine oozing sap, and, artfully poised above, two dry olive logs.

"Ignition," I said, frowning at Ellen, who had surreptitiously filled a bucket with water. "Three, two, one… liftoff!"

Where I used to live in North Carolina, they say that a good fireplace has to have a draft that will "Suck a cat off the hearthstone and blow him up the chimney." If your fireplace smokes, there's not a lot you can do about it but tear down some masonry and start over. I watched as the dark smoke from the kindling rose and dawdled at the top of the firebox, then as the *mata* caught fire and heat forced us back. When the sap wood caught, the smoke streamed straight up as if an exhaust fan was turned on full blast. The sides of the olive logs began to burn at once. The heat was too much for the mild morning, and I began to sweat. The domed hood around the smoke chamber quickly got too hot to touch.

"Put it on low, will you?" said Ellen.

Guisado stood back, mopping his head with a handkerchief. "It draws all right," he said reluctantly.

A sound began to issue from the fireplace. At first I thought I was imagining it, a kind of low moaning like wind on the shutters. As the flames built in the firebox, the sound increased. It rose in pitch and began to sound like a jet engine. Ellen jumped, and I turned to see a stack of loose newspaper fluttering in what was quickly becoming more than a breeze. The fire burned bright yellow. I could see shadows of our bodies on the opposite wall.

"*Hostia*," swore Guisado, stepping back.

"Look!" shouted Ellen. She was pointing to the carpet in front of the door to the kitchen, which had curled up ominously and then begun sliding toward the fireplace. I could feel wind at ankle height and see dust rising from the floor. I bent to separate the logs, to cool down the flame, when the door jumped its latch and flew open, slamming into the wall with a sickening crash of falling plaster. I tried to shut the door, but the draft was too strong for the latch.

"Put it out!" Ellen cried. "Put the fire out!"

Guisado threw the contents of the bucket into the firebox and black smoke and ash billowed into the room. The wailing of the fireplace stopped abruptly. A cloud of smoke hovered around the ceiling. I threw open a window. Behind me I heard Guisado's girlish laugh.

That afternoon I went back to the drawing board. Guisado went upstairs and threw more cement over the chimney, to reinforce it against the next blast. I hadn't counted on the rather narrow chimney rising twenty feet straight up. I hadn't realised that the overheated smoke chamber would suck so much air so quickly. I didn't need to worry about lack of draft. The fireplace would indeed suck a cat up the chimney. Maybe a German Shepherd, too.

Guisado was still smirking at the end of the day. I couldn't resist it, so I asked him innocently, "You wouldn't know where I could find some *setas,* would you?"

Revenge is sometimes sweet.

Chapter Thirteen

Driving Lessons

Aparicio sent word that he had found us a car. The next day we went up to Bill's farm and found him waiting in the drive with his son-in-law, Manuel, a carpenter and undertaker from Latigos. Carpenters are often also undertakers, since the main part of preparing for someone's last rites is the provision of a coffin. His van, painted a tasteful dark grey, did double duty as a hearse.

Manuel was leaning on an old red Seat 850 with sprayed-over rust on the fender wells and a missing hood ornament. It was a tiny car, second in tininess only to the legendary 650 that had gone out of production in the 1960's. The tires looked all right for retreads, and where the upholstery of the ceiling had started to droop, Manuel had applied silver gaffer tape. A medallion featuring the Virgin of Pilar swung from the rear view mirror.

Manuel didn't talk much. He was a handsome man whose smile was marred by a missing front tooth, the result, he claimed, of falling from an olive tree. I had explained to Aparicio that, because we were not yet Spanish residents, it wasn't legal for us to own a car. Manuel had agreed to remain in official ownership. He would let us have the car for 35,000 pesetas, about a hundred and fifty dollars. We were to pay for the insurance. Just in case there was any difficulty such as getting stopped by the Guardia Civil, he would write a note saying that we had borrowed the car. It was a familiar ruse that foreigners employed, and one tolerated by the police.

Even though we agreed at once, Manuel insisted on our taking the car for a spin, maybe in order to reassure himself that foreigners could drive. The four of us went up to Latigos, and I realised for the first time how narrow and twisting the roads really were. In all the three kilometres up the hill, there wasn't a single place to pull over. We left Manuel in front of his shop and took Aparicio back to Bill's.

I was feeling heady with power. Having a car meant that we could arrange for our own purchases of furniture and materials. We could go shopping in the lone supermarket in Ugijar. Best of all, we could have an occasional meal in a restaurant or even drive to the beach.

We began to learn the politics of car ownership the following morning, as we went into the plaza to buy some bread. Maria, the wife of the peon Jose, approached us near the fountain. She was someone we hardly knew, but her greeting was effusive.

She began by complaining to Ellen about Paqui's lack of stock in the shop. Without actually criticising her, she managed to convey the impression that Paqui only stocked goods that couldn't be sold in Ugijar. Apparently she currently had only two flavours of yoghurt, strawberry and lemon. She didn't like the one and the other gave her indigestion. Furthermore, the brand of powdered chicken stock she sold had no flavour and, what was more, she was once again out of fresh eggs. Ellen clucked her tongue non-committally. It wouldn't do to criticise Paqui, but Maria was speaking as if she were an intimate friend. I looked away; this was Ellen's problem, I thought.

Maria went on to ask if Ellen was aware that the semi-monthly market was being held in Ugijar the following day. There was a fellow there that had unbelievable bargains in things like *medias*, the short black nylon hose worn by every woman in the village over twenty. Ellen crossed her blue-jean clad legs over bare, sandaled feet. She cast me a look that pleaded for rescue, but I was busy looking at the ring of car keys in my hand.

"I don't suppose you're going to the market tomorrow, by any chance?" Maria said, and the point of this consumer awareness lecture finally dawned on me.

"Yes," I said. "Would you like a lift?"

The car we had bought would seat four passengers comfortably, and five at a pinch. By eleven o'clock we had agreed to take four people other than ourselves. We didn't mean to exceed our limit, but, after filling the seats, Guisado said that he needed to go because we needed to buy tiles for the kitchen or that he couldn't proceed with the work.

The next morning, as we stuffed passengers into the little car, a small crowd of villagers pressed around us. Paco Taxista, who had stayed at home in order to ferry people to the market, winked at me from across the plaza. As I crawled past him, car groaning on its springs, I shot him an apologetic look. I must be taking income away from him, I thought. He charged five hundred for the round trip, and I had two thousand in potential earnings on board.

He grinned. "Want a few more?" he asked, pointing to the scrum around his taxi. Partway down the mountain, as I gingerly shifted gears over someone's lap, he overtook us with a cheerful wave of his hand.

The next day we decided to branch out further. We had been curious about where all the men of the village went every morning. We knew that they worked in commercial greenhouses in a town called El Ejido, about two hours drive away. They travelled in private vans and on a chartered bus that parked each weeknight on a narrow strip of pavement in front of the schoolhouse. They were gone by the time we awoke, and only returned at dark. They could be seen in the bars, grimy-handed and fatigued. We had been told that if it were not for El Ejido there would be no Cantilla, since there was no place else to work.

"You want to see what Cantilla would look like without El Ejido?" asked Paco Junior one night in the bar. "Take a drive down to Lucainena." We had never heard of the place, but everyone nodded sagely. Why not, we thought, and one morning, hours after everyone else had left for work, we took a ride.

About five miles below Cantilla there is a bridge across the river as it winds through a deep canyon. It is probably better not to get a very good view of the bridge as you approach, preferring instead to admire the dense groves of oranges and lemons in the town of Cherin. Although the bridge is reputed to be very strong, one glance at the slender brick columns and arches from the 19th century is enough to worry anyone. I whistled, a tune from a musical Ellen dislikes, and managed to distract her. Midway across the bridge there is a rough patch of paving, and the worn springs of the Seat combined with this to give me a sudden thrill of terror.

Once across the bridge you are faced with a decision. To the left, a narrow but well-kept road heads for Berja, a large market town, and then to Almeria, on the coast. It is longer in distance to El Ejido, but shorter in journey time, or so we were told. To the right a narrow cut along a nearly sheer cliff face leads to the village of Lucainena, the place everyone said we should see. Stopped at the intersection, I could see that the road had no guard rails and was littered with fallen rocks. On the plus side, there was no traffic, and I calculated that there wasn't likely to be any, since Lucainena was now said to be a ghost town.

Ellen said, "Don't ask me. I'm not driving." I took this, typically, as a challenge, and we turned onto the road less travelled. At once it began to rise. I hugged the left side near the rock face when I could see ahead that nothing was approaching, leaving a good six feet between the car and the ragged edge of the road. We rounded the breast of a dry mountain, feeling encouraged. I began to relax, certain that at least the whole of the road was ours. I was still relaxed when an air horn blasted from yards away around a tight left hand bend.

I braked and skidded to a stop twenty feet from the chrome bumper of a passenger bus. We were so close that I could see the driver's gold tooth as he grimaced at us. All four sets of wheels of the bus were on the pavement, but passengers seated behind the driver were actually suspended over the sheer drop to the river. We eyeballed each other for a few seconds, until I heard the diesel engine die and the escape of air from the coach's brakes. The driver spoke briefly to the few passengers, who were leaning forward curiously, and squeezed out of the passenger side door onto the road. I shut off the engine. He approached us, looking, I thought, critically at our car, and leaned his head in my window.

"Where are yourselves going?" he asked, tapping out a cigarette from a packet of Ducados.

"Lucainena," I said. "Then on to El Ejido."

He shook his head. "The road from here on gets worse. You're better off turning around."

I was inclined to agree, but sitting in the middle of fifteen feet of broken asphalt halfway to the sky, I couldn't see how that was possible. The driver walked a few paces behind us down the road and scratched his neck, scowling. I was right; it wasn't possible to turn around.

"You'll have to reverse down to the next curve," he said. "Or else I can't get by."

I drive better going forward. Knowing this, I told Ellen to get out and walk beside the car to keep me well away from the edge. She hugged the side of the car when she saw what lay below her and kept close to the rock face as she gave me what I considered to be inadequate hand signals. The driver stalked impatiently past her to the curve we had just negotiated and waved his arm dramatically.

"Come on, come on," he called impatiently.

I started the car and eased out the clutch. This was difficult, because my left foot was disobeying, bobbing with a will of its own. The car lurched and stalled.

"Neutral!" shouted the driver. "Just let it coast." He grabbed the side mirror, as if he could hold the car away from the edge, and we crept backwards with little jerks as I pumped the brake. He jogged alongside, dragging at the mirror mount, shouting words of what I hoped were encouragement. Fifty yards or so along, he shouted for me to pull toward the inside of the curve, as close to the rock face as possible. I sat sweating in the car as

114

Ellen rejoined me, wisely saying nothing. We sat in silence as the coach appeared around the curve and hardly flinched as it squeezed so close to us that Ellen had to keep her arm inside to avoid a friction burn. Just clearing us, the coach suddenly picked up speed, as if expressing the driver's pique, and a final blast of the air horn shattered what was left of my nerve. He disappeared down the mountain.

"Don't say it," I warned.

"I'm mum," said Ellen.

The rest of the way to Lucainena was clear of traffic, if not of fallen rock obstacles and long views of different ways to die. I got some of my confidence back when I saw that we were entering the outskirts of the village. The drop to our right gradually became a gentle slope leading down to terraces of olive trees that led to the river. A large farmhouse sat perched on the cliff above us. Its porch columns were leaning and the earth in front of the building had given way, causing it to sag crazily. Then a row of houses, shuttered and peeling paint. As we rounded a bend, a church of unplastered brick loomed over a narrow plaza planted with untended plane trees. We parked and stood in front of the church on a stone paved patio with a low wall overlooking the valley.

There was no one in sight. A few faded pennants from a bygone fiesta hung from the electricity wires. Houses stood, clearly intact if wanting a touch of paint. A few strings of drying peppers from some past harvest swung in someone's *camara*. There was no sound except a whisper of the hot wind and the distant rush of the river. We walked through what had been, not too long before, a good-sized village, with fruit and olive trees on well maintained terraces. Weeds, dried by the summer past, stood where there had obviously been gardens and fields of corn. The feeling was not, as I had expected, eerie, but a little sad, like seeing a pair of a dead man's shoes. The signs of the little eccentricities of each family's way of living were poignant. In one courtyard, shaded by an overgrown grape arbour, a baby's pram stood, its fabric rotting and flapping in the wind. In front of another was an old car resting wheelless on blocks. The bonnet was up and the engine had been removed.

Lucainena, after a thousand years of history, had found itself in the watershed of a new dam project. Because the waste of houses and fields drained into the planned catchment area of a dam six miles away, the people, their animals and their waste products had had to be removed. After years of argument and court battles, the citizens had been compensated and re-located downhill near Berja. A few, however, mostly old people, had refused to go. At the time we went there, there were still six old women resident in the village. Their lawyers had ensured that they could live out their natural life spans in their homes. And because this made it still an occupied village, the government had found itself required to keep on providing services for their homes. There was a postal delivery every day, street lights were kept functioning, garbage picked up and water flowing, and even—as we had discovered—a once-per-day bus service.

We walked through the empty streets hoping to see one of the old people we had heard were still in residence, but they were keeping to themselves. The only sign of human occupation was damp clothing hanging on a wash line across rooftop of an empty house. And once we thought we heard the ghostly barking of a dog.

A village is more than houses, more than people. Every village of the Alpujarras has a history. This history is embodied above all in the sacramental objects held in the church. In some cases these were relics, such as the hair clippings of a saint, or even, we were told, the occasional piece of *la vera cruz*, the true cross. These relics, whether the village physically existed or not, were the sign of its continuing presence. Outside the deserted church stood a new cement building, windowless and locked with a stout-looking steel door. A sign said that this was the property of the diocese of Almeria. No doubt the village's Virgin statue, the musty holy cloths used to drape her for processions, and who knew what other relics were safely locked inside.

Downstream from Lucainena there had been another village, Beninar, but it was now submerged under the water of the new dam. All the buried bones from the churchyard had been relocated to a nearby hill and marked with the traditional planting of cypress trees. The relics of Beninar had been kept there as well. Each year, at the traditional time of the fiesta honouring the Virgin deemed the patron of that place, those who remained of the population still gathered for a party. As time passed, there were fewer and fewer people left, until only the very elderly attended. But Beninar still existed as long as this tradition was maintained.

We drove to Berja, past the new reservoir-- low and unnaturally green with fertiliser effluent from the nearby farms-- down a road newly paved and tended. As we neared the town, we saw what at first seemed to be an inlet of the sea. Then we realised that these were our first *invernaderos,* acre-sized greenhouses of wire and plastic, home to chemical-flooded dead soil and tomatoes and other salad crops packed together like battery chickens. The light reflected off the flapping roofs cast a dead glow over the valley, turning even the deep blue Alpujarran sky to a cold white. I parked and we looked out over the valley below, trying to imagine how it had been before somebody had had a bright idea about how to make some money.

We turned the car around in silence. There was no need to go to El Ejido; we knew what we'd find there. I knew that these agricultural hells were necessary to pay the people who live in places like Cantilla, and that if you really must have strawberries in January in Edinburgh, this is the price you have to pay. Somehow it didn't help.

"Thank God Cantilla's too high up for these things, that's all I've got to say," I told Ellen. She nodded but didn't answer.

Chapter Fourteen

Power Struggles

We stopped to do some shopping in Ugijar, and so got back to Cantilla just as dusk was settling. Ellen went home with the groceries. I went to the Plaza bar and found Paco Junior setting up for the evening rush.

Paco Junior was a youngish man with a permanently serious expression that marked his position of authority in the village. As the proprietor of the single most important institution in Cantilla, he had to appear formal, even forbidding. If you wanted to find someone, he could tell you where they were. If you needed a postage stamp or a bottle of butane gas, he could do that for you. If you wanted to pay your electric bill or fill out a tax form, he could help you. He played a radio at all times, keeping it at low volume so that only he could hear it, because, as he told me, he wasn't licensed for music. Mostly he tuned in to news broadcasts, which made him easily the best-informed person in town. When he was concentrating, his brow furrowed in a way that made him seem all the more unapproachable, but though he brooked no rowdy behaviour from customers, I learned quickly that he was gifted with a sharp sense of humour that sometimes passed over the heads of the drinkers leaning against the bar. I liked to catch him early, before the men returned from the day's work.

"What do you think about *Otan*?" he asked me suddenly, as he cracked open a bottle of beer for me.

"Pardon?"

"*Otan*. You know, the North Atlantic Treaty Organisation."

"Oh, *Nato*." I was flustered. "I don't think about it very much, I guess."

He frowned. "You should take more interest in politics, Arturo."

"Well, Nato's been around longer than I have," I said. "What do you think about it?"

He leaned on the bar, pointing a finger at me. I recognised this as a rhetorical device rather than an accusation. "If Spain joins Otan," he said darkly, "Then Spain will have to go to war with anyone who invades America."

"Yes," I said placatingly, "But America will have to go to war with anyone who invades Spain."

"Aha!" he said triumphantly. "But no one wants to invade Spain. We have no enemies."

"I see what you mean."

"On the other hand," he continued, wiping the counter as if clearing away enemies, "No one would be foolish enough to invade America."

"I guess not," I said, straining to catch his point.

"So?"

"So, what?"

Paco Junior sighed at my deplorable political consciousness. "So, should Spain join Otan?"

"Maybe so, maybe not," I said, finally getting the point.

"Exactly!" He smiled. "It's important to consider these things carefully."

"I couldn't agree more."

A few men were filing into the bar. I recognised Jose, the brother of my neighbour, Francisco. He greeted me warmly. I thought this must be because we had now bonded through the sale of the house. I asked how his work in the *invernaderos* was going.

"It's work," he said cheerfully.

"Francisco doesn't go with you, does he?" I asked carefully, digging.

"Francisco? Work?" He exchanged a smile with Paco Junior.

"It's because of his eye, right?" I continued. "Some kind of accident at work?"

Jose winked broadly at Paco. "Arturo wants to know if Francisco hurt his eye at work." He gave me a nudge. "Depends what you call work, eh, Paco?" He laughed out loud. "That depends on the work."

He ate a meatball that Paco Junior had slid in front of him and threw the toothpick on the floor.

"Do you want to hear what happened to my brother?" he asked, and without waiting for an answer, told me.

One evening two years before, Francisco was seated, as usual, at the kitchen table while Mari cooked his dinner. He had had a few glasses of wine, as was customary. Without warning a large stray cat that lived on the rooftops of the neighbourhood, who was rumoured to weigh ten kilos and be over thirty years old, jumped onto the table, seized a sausage of *longaniza* in its jaw and shot down the stairs. Enraged, Francisco sprang after him. Reaching the first landing, he was amazed to see that the beast had stopped, arched his back and was hissing menacingly at him. Startled, he tripped and fell all the way to the ground floor, striking his head and losing consciousness.

Francisco could not be roused, even with a loving bucket of water thrown over him by Mari. She and the eldest son carried and dragged him to the plaza, to her sister's house. When it was seen that blood was trickling from both ears, the Guardia Civil was notified and an ambulance summoned. He was taken to Granada to the hospital. Mari rode with him, but returned the following day to report that Francisco had fallen into a deep coma and was not expected to live. Everyone was shocked. All the teasing they had done about his poetry and his dislike of work was retracted over tearful and copious glasses of wine. Mari, always practical, instructed Manuel, the undertaker of Latigos, to begin making a coffin.

Francisco lay unconscious for six days, connected to tubes and pumps in a room reserved for terminal cases. On the seventh morning, a nurse entered his room to find him wandering in circles, fully conscious but complaining of dizziness. He asked politely for a small glass of wine, just to clear his head. Tests were performed. He had sustained damage to his brain, but apart from one small difficulty, he was as good as new: he could only use one eye at a time. He had acquired permanent double vision that robbed him of balance when looking out of both eyes.

He returned to Cantilla a few days later, wearing a new pair of glasses with a flesh-coloured patch over one lens. He was happily clutching a document that declared him to be permanently disabled, entitled to benefit payments and, even better, officially unable to work. He told the story over and over in the bar, obligingly removing his glasses and falling over to demonstrate his disability. He had achieved at an early age what many poets long for, a guaranteed income.

For a year Francisco drew his benefits, each day faithfully changing the patch from one eye to the other as the doctors had instructed, in order to preserve the vision in each. At the end of the year he was required to report for a routine examination of his case to a social worker in Granada. He travelled down on the day of his appointment in Paco's taxi, but was unavoidably detained by meeting a few old friends from his seminary days in a bar. He arrived at the end of the day, just as the social worker was finishing his appointments. He was told gruffly to report the following morning at eight o'clock sharp. The social worker's demeanour puzzled Francisco, since he himself was in a jolly frame of mind.

Paco Taxista got him there ten minutes early the next morning. Francisco was first in line. As he entered the office, the social worker looked at him suspiciously.

"Didn't you have that patch on your other eye yesterday?" he asked imperiously, but before Francisco could explain, he found himself being ejected from the interview. As he slammed the door in his face, the social worker hissed at Francisco that, due to his attempt to defraud the government, his benefits were being stopped immediately. If he wanted them renewed, he would have to appeal to a judge. The stipend had been ended through the impenetrable workings of fate.

Francisco, a basically optimistic man, remained cheerful, though his credit dried up at the bar. He wrote a series of florid letters that received no replies. Recently, said Jose, he had found a new lawyer, his third, who had promised to get the benefits restored. Meanwhile, Mari, a stoic like her mother, was the sole breadwinner. She worked alongside the men of the pueblo each day, while Francisco minded the children.

Jose shook his head. "He wasn't working, anyway, when he fell. But since then he only talks about one thing. That damned cat."

That night I carefully lit a fire in the new fireplace. I had learned to keep it low and to build the blaze as near as possible to the back wall. In a flash of inspiration I had hacked a hole in the floor just in front of the hearth, so that incoming air would be drawn from the corral below, and not through the house. The nights were chilly now. As soon as the sun went down you needed a sweater. Satisfied that the fire would burn safely all night, I went to bed.

Fading, my mind turned to Francisco and the story of his accident. I reminded myself not to mention the cat to Ellen. The Demon Cat, as I now thought of it. It wouldn't do for her to think I was getting paranoid from culture shock. The grizzled visage of the animal stuck in my mind, accompanying me down into sleep. I would have dreamed of him, I am sure, if the face of Agustina hadn't suddenly swum into view, tight-lipped and frozen in grief.

I sat bolt upright in bed. Emilio, her doomed husband, had fallen, over twenty years ago and no one had ever discovered why. I got up and paced the lounge. Sleep was forgotten.

Could that damned cat really be that old?

Chapter Fifteen

A Good Person

I had become a *buena persona*.

I found this out one afternoon in the Plaza Bar by accident. I had spent the day helping Bill and Aparicio plant some new fruit trees. With the increasingly cold nights, Aparicio had deemed it time to do grafting and planting. Bill would have a fruit orchard of apples, peaches and pears. The whips went into holes into which we had put stones and a good mixture of topsoil and manure from the goat house. They stood in rows a little farther apart than was necessary, because Bill would put annual row crops in between. When they were all planted, Aparicio opened a plastic bag he had put on the far edge of the terrace.

"What's in there?" I asked him.

"Dog shit," he replied, deadpan.

"Come on, what is it really?"

"I told you. Dog shit. The best I could find in Latigos, where the dogs eat better than the people of Cantilla do."

He mixed some dry red powder from a tin and some water in a bucket and added the contents of the bag. The combined smells were horrible. Even the dogs hung back. Aparicio mixed it into a slurry, grinning at me. He took a paint brush from his hip pocket and handed me the bucket.

"Arturo, you paint this on the trees. From the ground up to the first branch."

"You must be joking," I said.

Shrugging, Aparicio started painting the trees, which now turned a sickening orange.

"It's to keep the goats from eating the bark," Bill said, taking two brushes from the porch. He handed me one. "It's the only way."

Nothing is wasted in the Alpujarras.

When I got to Paco's bar I went straight to the toilet and scrubbed my hands. Twice. I wasn't really squeamish, just careful. When I came out I nearly bumped into two policemen from the *Guardia Civil* post, three-cornered hats stuffed under the arms of their green uniforms. Images of the Franco era crowded into my mind. In those days, you avoided the civil guards if you could. They were the enforcers of the dictator's puritanical regime. They had sometimes thrown backpacking foreigners into jail for offences that were not well defined, and had been known to give enforced haircuts to people they thought were a little too shaggy for the Catholic tastes of the authorities. We had called them "Mickey Mouseketeers" because of the odd patent leather hats they wore, but never so that they could hear. Even now, in the post-Franco liberal regime of the left-of-centre government, they could raise a little ridge of atavistic hairs on my neck.

"Is this the one?" said one of the cops to Paco, who nodded.

"*Buenas tardes*," I said casually. I had intended to have a beer, but my thirst had vanished. I strolled by as casually as possible, but their postures indicated that they wanted to have a word with me. I stopped, feeling caught. I realised that there were any number of small offences I had committed by the very fact of my presence.

"Your passport, please, *Senor*," said one of them, an unsmiling tall fellow with glasses.

"I can give you a photocopy. That's all I carry with me, but the original is in my house," I said.

The officer took the creased and grimy paper I handed him. The other looked on expressionlessly. He took his time reading it, then removed a notebook from his pocket and made a few notes. I kept a smile on my face with some effort.

"You live in this village now?" he asked at last. Recognising this question as the first in a minefield, I said,

"Live, no. We are vacationing here. A holiday." This was in case the issue of residence came up. Technically we could remain in Spain for six months without residence visas, providing we didn't work. But since the border guards never stamped passports of North American and European countries these days, it was not really enforceable.

"But you have bought a house, no?"

"Yes. Just a small one," I said, lamely.

"And your wife?"

"She is at home."

He handed me my photocopy, nodded and then turned back to the bar. I noticed with displeasure that Paco had opened a

127

bottle of beer for me and placed it on the counter near the police. I raised my eyebrows beseechingly, and he slid it to the other end of the bar. Trapped, I amused myself by reading the calendar on the wall behind the bar, which was virtually the only item of decoration. The cops talked to each other, and occasionally Paco joined in. I could catch some of what they were saying. There was a worrying influx of hippies in Los Monteros, a village to the south. Most of these were Spanish, but there were foreigners as well. School kids in Ugijar had been caught carrying drugs. Last week a routine stop check of a car at a rural crossroad yielded the seizure of a boot full of hashish. A pair of Moroccans had held up a branch bank in a coastal town.

The local people tolerated the *Civiles* because they were the only police around. The national police only operate in cities, and municipal cops, with the exception of one bored man in Ugijar, didn't exist. There were those that didn't feel so enthusiastic, such as old Jose, who had spent three years in a roofless prison cell after the civil war. He remembered being marched to church at gunpoint by the *Guardia,* who were enforcing Franco's pledge to the priests to strengthen the church. In general, *Civiles* fitted in with local culture, although by policy, they were never stationed near their places of origin, and were therefore not Andalucians. Because they were exotic, and wore uniforms, they were attractive to local girls. There had been more than one case of unhappy affairs and broken marriages. People like Paco Junior, who was interested in everything, used them as a source of information for his philosophical barmanship.

Lapsing in to a reverie at the bar, I suddenly realised that the conversation had turned to me. I caught sight of the second cop pointing surreptitiously in my direction. The other cop laughed. Paco Junior, his face even more earnest than usual, was saying "something, something….*buena persona…*

something, something… no problem." I nearly blushed. He was talking about me. I was a *buena persona*. The cops were nodding. When they turned to leave, they gave me a kind of offhand salute of *adios*.

I asked Paco why they had been asking about me. He replied that it was their job to keep track of foreigners in the area. Since Ellen and I were the only ones in Cantilla they hadn't had to stay very long. I gathered up my courage and asked,

"Why does everybody call us hippies?"

Paco looked puzzled. "Aren't you?"

"My mother would hate that."

"Well, Arturo," he said, looking a touch embarrassed, "That's what people call foreigners around here. Hippies don't have jobs, they don't drive big cars or wear suits like the Americans and English on the telly."

I explained that where I was from, hippies were basically extinct, but the few remaining museum pieces from the sixties hung around places like Ibiza and Amsterdam. We didn't drive big cars or wear suits because we were poor, and anyway, didn't like them all that much. I also couldn't seem to explain exactly what we were doing here now. It wasn't a matter of culture, but a kind of missing piece in my own head, one that Ellen sometimes seemed to want to talk about. I don't think Paco caught my meaning, but I decided I didn't mind. I was a hippie, but I was now, officially, a *buena persona*.

If Paco Junior thought I was a good person, that was that. Not that his influence was so great, but because I had come to realise that places like Cantilla tend to form group opinions. If you came one morning into the plaza feeling slightly chilly, you might remark to someone that the day had a nip to it. If group opinion concurred with your analysis, they would agree; "Yes, today is cold." If not, you would be corrected: "No, today is not cold; it is warmer than yesterday." That would be the universal judgement on the weather, and try though you might to find a dissenter, everyone in the village would agree. The same was true of almost any phenomenon. If someone says that so-and-so is a greedy person, then that was so, and everyone knew it. Something like that had happened to Guisado, and the reverse, it seemed, had just happened to me.

I can't say where these group opinions originate, or how. It would be possible to imagine a cabal formed of a few weighty citizens meeting in the pre-dawn hours to form the day's opinions and disseminate them before breakfast. Or, perhaps, some form of Jungian synchronicity, operating telepathically on everyone within the town limits. All I can say is that I never saw it fail. It might be useful to remember that the Spanish word for village is *pueblo*, which also means "people." I had already begun to realise that when Ellen and I bought a house, we had done much more without knowing it. We had joined a community that shared more than real estate. We were enmeshed in a psychic web of humanity that went back a thousand years.

Feeling humbled, as if I had just been given the keys to the city, I walked home. A few kids called out as I passed them, "'*turo!*" They had been doing this for a while, and I had come to like it. I was the only person named Arturo they had ever met. It seems that many of them, because of the peculiarities of the local accent, thought my name was "Alturo." This would mean something like "tall." Because I was a head taller than most of the men in the village, this made a kind of sense.

Alturo, hippie and *buena persona*, was at home in Cantilla. I couldn't wait to tell Ellen.

The next day I walked to Bill's by the path along the *asequia*. Ellen seemed a little moody, and, as often these days, stayed home. I knew that she must be beginning to have questions about our being here, questions that had been ignored in the rush to make a home. We had learned from our entries into the poor villages where we had been working how to get to know people, how to watch the elements of culture unfold without making quick judgements. We had done the same thing in Cantilla, except, this time, we had no assignment, no sending agency, no *raison d'etre*. I had always seemed to feel comfortable around so-called "primitive" cultures. It may have been a kind of idealistic fixation on the nobility of uncorrupted peoples, a Rousseauvian hang-up. The problem was, "noble savages" always seemed to be just waiting for a chance to develop motorways, over-consumption and stress diseases. The idea of noble poverty was hard to sustain in places where people didn't have shoes and the children died of curable diseases. But with my usual blend of optimism and cheerful ignorance, I managed to ignore this reality as long as possible. I wasn't so sure about Ellen, who for all her artistic gifts, still had a fairly hard-boiled view of life. I brushed the thoughts away and turned my attention to the path to Bill's.

To reach the path you balance on a narrow strip of cement that juts unexpectedly from the village past a chicken house guarded by a pair of anti-social dogs. The dogs seem not to know who is a *buena persona.* They will court the very edge of misbehaviour, defined as actually biting a fellow Cantillero, although people from Latigos would be fair game. It is not easy to do a balancing act while avoiding yellow teeth and canine attitude. Once past their territory, you can express your true feelings with a stone if you can find one.

The *asequia* bends along the curve of a hill above a garden lined with lemon trees and divided by a stream. The going is easier there on the wide ribbon of concrete. You begin to ascend along the slope of the watercourse, past a hump of land covered in prickly pears where the irrigation doesn't reach. At the next bend, a sharp one to the left, the *acequia* goes its own way, and you follow a path past a *cortijo* in an orange grove. If you stop and turn around here, you will see the whole of Cantilla. There will be a few women hanging out clothes on their flat rooftops, the domain of the village cats, high and safe from dogs. A tethered mule will be grazing, tail twitching, in the gardens below the veranda. At this time of year, when the nights are sharp, you will see old men tending buckets of fire at the doorways. They are making *ascuas*, or coals, for the braziers under the tables. It is olive wood, and it takes all day. Truant children may be seen helping with agricultural chores. They keep one eye on the toddlers, who run fearlessly between the legs of the mules and horses.

The path leads you along the tops of terraces of olives, just now ripening green and black in the branches. There is a tree so old that the trunk is thicker than three children's arm's reach, and so gnarled and pitted with history that it has been lovingly guyed with strong baling wire to the terrace above. It has been falling for many years, and the wire has disappeared into the bark. The ground is wet here; a small spring oozes beneath the olive tree and makes mud of the path.

At the end of the cultivated land the trail is steeper. It narrows to a single-file track as it breasts a rise and then descends suddenly into a *barranco* where an immense chestnut tree blocks out the sunlight. Here you can make a bad decision. The better trail leads off downhill to a deserted mill near the river. You must take the one that looks less likely if you want to get to Bill's. A few steps dug into a bank lead you onto a terrace belonging to Paco Taxista. This is not well-tended, since his day job keeps him away a lot. Another bend to the left and you enter a world that seems very far from the village. The view across the river is of a cliff-like slope where trees cling with knotted roots to the rock and *chumbos* project against gravity in mid-air.

You rejoin the *acequia*, now rising swiftly through chiselled rock to its source in the mountains above. The path is narrow, and you use your arms for balance like a tightrope walker. Gradually the sound of the river reaches your ears. As you round the next bend it becomes a roar. You would like to watch the white water as it pours over a series of rock dams, where trout spend the dry summer months in deep wells. But you keep your eyes on the trail, because falling here means a long tumble to the river. To the left is a wall of slate, where men have found paving stones for centuries. It rises over your head, rust-brown and crumbling, and slabs fall onto the path. Just here there is a cut in the stone like a steep staircase. If you take it you will avoid the brambles below Bill's farm a few hundred metres along. It is a scramble, but when you reach the top you are standing on a shelf of flat rock from which you can see all the way to Lucainena, and, beyond that, to the sea. Bill's dogs will bark at that precise moment, and then come charging into the open, glad of something to do. If you crane your neck you may see Aparicio leaning over the top terrace wall by the garden. The dogs will escort you the rest of the way.

I had just crossed the muddy place beneath the chestnut tree, and was climbing winded onto Paco's terrace when I ran into a flock of sheep and goats. They were grazing the weeds beneath the olive trees. The goats had risen up what seemed to be a sheer bank and stood gnawing bark off shrubs growing from the rock. A large dog with docked ears and tail stood among them. He was fixing me with an unkind stare and not wagging his tail. I made kissing noises to call him to me, but he just growled. His owner leaned against the trunk of an olive tree with something like the same expression. He was a youngish man with a Fidel Castro cap and a leather bag strapped across his military-style tunic like a Sam Brown belt. He had a bandit's moustache that curled down nearly to his chin, and eyes so dark they looked black.

133

I recognised him as Rafael, the brother of a man I sometimes spoke with in the bar. He was considered to be *pesado*, "heavy." This word was used for people who, though not quite violent, were threatening in their aspect. When sober, he was quiet and stern of countenance. When drunk, everyone left him alone.

I had realised that shepherds bore an unusual relationship to the other members of the village. Because of their work, they spent little time in the company of others. In days past, they had ranged so far afield that they often slept rough in the countryside. There are many little shelters and caves where you can see evidence of their fires. Because they slept rough, they were unshaven and unkempt, adding an element of wildness to their appearance. Brushing against their animals all day, and milking after dark, they smelled of lanolin, that product so loved by cosmetics manufacturers that actually smells sharply unpleasant. Rumours of their sexual misconduct added an aura of decadence to their image. Jokes about bestiality were standard fare in the bars. There was an unmistakable resemblance to the horny god Pan, as well, the archetype feared and loved by women.

Rafael looked at me with studied insolence. He ignored my cheerful greeting. He took a *navaja*, hunting knife, from his pocket and began whittling a stick into a point. The sheep were enclosing me, and the black dog stared with the vigilance of a watchman. I felt an edge of unease, something short of actual fear, that was incongruous in this ordinary morning.

"Alturo," he said in a voice made mossy by his forest life. "Alturo the foreigner."

"That's me," I said, making my voice chipper. His flat expression made me regret it.

"Where's Alturo going, then? Out here in the woods."

"To see Bee," I said, and pointed along the path.

"Give me a cigarette," said Rafael. He didn't say "please."

"I don't smoke," I said. Alongside the unease I could feel something else, like anger. What was this clown up to?

He took a packet of Ducados from his bag and lit one with a butane lighter. His eyes never left mine. I pushed forward against the sheep and made a wide arc around him toward the path.

"Whoa, Alturo." he said, "Don't scare my sheep." He pushed off from his leaning position on the tree. The dog tensed and made a throaty low rumble. "Foreigners don't know how to treat sheep, do they?" I wondered if he had heard about my arrival in Latigos the year before. It made me feel a little weaker in this undeclared showdown.

I ignored him and made for the path. The dog barked twice. My palms felt wet. I thought about picking up a stone, but kept moving. He stayed where he was, but the dog moved in my direction. I stopped and faced him. This was getting stupid. I had had some fairly dry encounters with people of the Alpujarras, but nearly everyone treated me with friendliness. I knew that whatever game of nerves he was playing, it wouldn't be approved of in the village. I had a fifty-pound weight advantage, easily. He had a knife and a useful looking stick, not to mention the dog.

"Call your dog, Rafael," I said.

There was a spell of silence. It seemed longer than it was. There was a lot going on that we weren't saying. He knew it and so did I. I leaned on my anger, which is a much more pleasant emotion than fear. Rafael must have felt it. He called the dog, and when it didn't respond, gave it a hard whack with the stick that sent it whimpering behind him. He said nothing to me, but smiled in a way that didn't involve his eyes at all. I gave him a five count, then turned and walked unhurriedly up the path and around the corner. It wasn't until I was almost to Bill's that I realised I was trembling.

Bill was, as usual, unexcited. "You can't expect everybody to like you, you know." he said.

"But I'm a *buena persona*," I joked. "Ask Paco Junior."

"Cantilleros,"Aparicio muttered.

That night I went home by the road.

Chapter Sixteen

Slaughter

When it is time for the annual slaughter in Cantilla, this is how it happens. It is a Saturday, and the men have stayed home. All day long they have been at it, gathering expectantly in mute clusters at corners and wide places in the village streets. Kids are not going so far from home, and the dogs, whose duties often carry them miles away, are snuffling humbly around the legs of the women. These have been here since early morning. They have built great olive wood fires under huge vats of water. Steam rises white into the blue margins of the sky. For once the men are not grumbling about the lack of rain. It is a cold, clear Saturday in December, and they are going to kill the pigs.

Perhaps it is the season that gives this sense of expectation. The air bites a little in the mornings. The people haven't bothered much with fresh litter for the pigs under the houses recently, and there is a harsh putridity at certain doorways. There have been last efforts to add fat to the *marrano*, the pig, at this late hour. People have been liberal with the unshelled maize that has been drying in the open attics.

The architecture has changed. Thick poles have emerged from the lofts and been placed, attic to attic, across the streets. The strands of drying red peppers which have been here all autumn are retired, but the racks made of cane still remain like flag standards across the house front, waiting for the gleaming lengths of *morcilla*, blood sausage.

At about four o'clock, men—specialists—can be seen entering the village from the highway. They are in-laws and cousins and friends whose skill is killing the pigs. They wear green gum boots and blue boiler suits. From their belts hang a hook with a handle, and they carry long grooved knives. Their coming is greeted excitedly, but they remain aloof, as if to invest their tasks with solemnity.

At the killing places tables have appeared. These measure exactly 105 centimetres in length and 75 in width and are 70 centimetres above the ground. They are made of mulberry wood, olive and *almes*. They have probably always been the same. They are very strong, as they need to be. Some foreigners buy them for charming kitchen tables when they can find a carpenter willing to make one, but the villagers use them just once a year, for the *matanza*.

Kids alert the clusters that the butcher has arrived, moving in telepathic sympathy with the other clusters up the streets, sensing everything an instant before the adults. Dogs are banished with a few well-timed kicks. The women, wearing their worst old clothes and head rags, move back. The men go forward to meet the butcher.

Things move quickly. A delegation, including the householder, vanishes into the corral. A rope is tied to the foreleg of the pig, and he is coerced and dragged into the street, letting out the first of an accelerating series of disconcertingly human-like squeals. The excitement rises; dogs whimper in greed and sympathy from their places of banishment. The pig, blinking, sees the sky for the first time since last April, when he was an infant. He grows calmer again as the expectant circle readies itself. As the men move forward, the pig senses exactly what is about to happen, with that prescience that you can almost always see on the faces of prisoners.

The knot of men closes on the pig, surprisingly long and pink under its sparse hair. He turns into the rope and fouls his foreleg. The butcher steps forward, concealing the hook behind his thigh like a matador (for that is what he is) and suddenly catches the pig underneath his jaw with its sharp point. The squeal rises in volume. The pig resists. Its human eyes sweep the crowd as it is hauled like a fish off its front feet. The other men close in, fumbling for a handhold on the 200-pound bulk. Seizing hair, tail, knee, they drag it on its side onto the table. The wails are now continuous. The butcher spits instructions, but the men can hardly hear them. A leg is bound and tied to the table. Two men lean their full weight upon the hams; another pair hang from a rope hastily pulled across the pig's belly. There is something almost furtive about their movements. It is easy to imagine guilt beneath their tight faces.

Once the pig is firmly tied, it is allowed to grow calm. Only its eyes show its terror, darting back and forth across the crowd, searching for the source of danger. This is now in the deft hand of the butcher, who turns his back and gives the blade a few ceremonial swipes across a whetstone. On this cue, the woman of the house comes forward with a metal basin. It is placed on the road downward and to the left of the pig's frantic eye.

The matador cuts slowly, inserting the knife with the finesse of a surgeon looking for a vein in a patient. This is exactly what he is doing. Once sure he has found the jugular, he presses the haft of the knife with the heel of his hand. It slides inward easily. All at once, the pig knows. Its great bulk surges against the weight of the men and undulates like a wave. A scream begins; the butcher leans back against the pull of the hook and stretches the jaw forward. A jet of bright blood spurts out, overshoots the basin, which is hurriedly adjusted. The force of the blood makes a metallic drone as it flows. The pig's cries are now rhythmic, and the rate ebbs and flows with its movements. The pan fills rapidly.

The pig, it is clear, feels no special pain. Its dismay is cosmic, and something of its despair is communicated to everyone. There is no talking except for the rushed instructions of the butcher. I have seen slaughters in other places where the animal has been mocked, and a carnival air prevailed as in a witches' Sabbath. Here there is no frivolity. Even the dogs and children are subdued. They are in the presence of something profound. What is before them is a paradox that only ends, but is never resolved.

The flow weakens. There is a glaze on the pig's visible eye. As the last of his blood flows out, all can see him die. It happens quite suddenly, and always the same thing happens. The body, abandoned, exerts its earthy force in a single long spasm. The men half climb onto the pig to constrain it as it nearly jack-knifes, give a long rippling shudder, and is still. A boy actually is heard to say, "*Adios, Marranico*."

The mood shifts. They are one fewer now. The pig has been transformed into meat, a huge and worrying quantity of meat. Hurry rules the crowd. The women join the men, pouring boiling water onto the flesh, scraping with the sharpened edge of a tablespoon. The scraping noises intersperse with excited conversation. Soon the pig is bare. Except for one single act, the dividing of the carcass into sections, the women now take over. They move forward eagerly. You can feel the sexual power shift as the carcass is hauled into the air and left swinging from the poplar poles. The entrails spill out into a plastic tub. The women will heal this pig now, deliver it from its condition of alienation into *morcilla*, *chorizo*, ham and bacon. It is almost part of their children and men already; you can see it in their eyes.

They will not sleep tonight. There are onions to peel, great sacks of them, spices to express, blood to boil, links to tie. Tomorrow you will see them, crusty with meat, hoarse and sweaty and strong, in the plaza, laughing from their state of sleepless intoxication and joy. They are so powerful that the men, slow with a night's feasting, avoid them. This could be a day to redress old wrongs.

We had been hearing ominous rumblings, like rumours of war. There was a look of anticipation on people's faces that had nothing to do with Christmas. The smell at doorways was indeed getting a little harsh, and people were carrying extra maize into their corrals. Householders looked at the sky, waiting this time not for rain but for the first cold night, when the flies would be dead at last. We knew in our bones what was going to happen. They were going to kill the pigs.

"Forget it," said Ellen, on the first really chilly morning. "Call me a hypocrite, but I like my meat in little plastic packages, not covered with hair and begging for mercy."

"You're a hypocrite."

141

"Good. That's what you can tell Francisco and Mari, then, 'Sorry, neighbours, but Ellen can't help you murder your pig, as she is indisposed with hypocrisy.'"

"What *am* I going to tell them? It's all Francisco talks about, except for the Cat."

She sighed, I thought a little dramatically. "You know what your problem is, Art? You can't stand not being popular. So you'll go and do God knows what to that poor animal just so the men won't think you're a foreigner. Which, by the way..."

"Okay, so I'm a foreigner. That doesn't mean dumping on their customs. Francisco has asked me especially to help with the, uh, slaughter, and I'm not going to let him down."

Thus began an uneasy truce. We pointedly did not open the kitchen window, where outside Mari and Concha, her sister-in-law, had been boiling water all day in a huge metal cauldron. We could not just slip away to Bill's, because the women were directly in front of our door. Francisco and Jose were at their kitchen table, arguing and laughing over a bottle of wine. Their voices sounded coarse, even reckless. Despite what I had said to Ellen, I was full of dread.

I was sitting at the kitchen table when the inevitable pounding came on the front door. Ellen was in the living room, listening to the stereo. This was because she was sure that the pig would make some noises at the critical moment, and she did not intend to hear them. I went down and opened the door. Francisco, already the worse for wear from celebrating, weaved in the doorway.

"Okay, Arturo," he said merrily, "Let's finish the *marrano*."

It was both better and worse than I had expected. The pig went quickly, as if he had always really known this was going to happen, and there was no mockery or visible bloodlust among the neighbours. But as the animal began his journey to the other world, he did make some disconcertingly human-like squeals. I heard Ellen turn up the volume on the stereo. The

142

pig departed to the strains of Elgar's *Nimrod*. In twenty minutes he was hanging in two sections from a pole stretched across the street.

I had realised quickly why I was such a valued helper at the slaughter. It wasn't my cool head or manual co-ordination; it was my weight. Once the pig is on his table, someone that weighs a lot has to lie across his body, pinning his hefty free ham down to avoid being kicked by a useful-looking hoof. That was me. The much smaller men of the pueblo admired my physical size. It was just a little disappointing.

Ellen met me at the door. I thought she was going to embrace me sympathetically after my brave ordeal, but she had another motive.

"Leave that shirt down here," she said crossly. "You're not bringing pig shit into my kitchen."

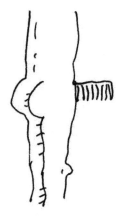

Chapter Seventeen

Fluency

The incident had intensified a feeling I was having these days. When you're a learner, as we were, absorbing the culture of the village, the country and the language, it is possible to feel a little helpless. The other men around me were at home in their world. They knew all about building terraces, irrigation and plants. They were at ease as they passed a mule tethered across the street, and they never ran the risk of being kicked. They could work all day in the greenhouses and come back and drink until the wee hours. They even had a name for it, a word they used all the time. *Apanado.* We had to look it up in the big dictionary.

It means "handy or capable." It was the highest compliment you could pay another man. You shook your head respectfully and said, "He's *apanado*." I knew that Ellen felt much the same about the women, with their strong arms and gutsy manner. She was full of admiration for people who could hoist a load of olive logs onto their shoulder while carrying a baby under the other arm, and sing *cante hondo* as they were doing it. But, unlike me, she didn't seem to mind being put in this inferior position. I wanted to be *apanado*, too.

"Male ego," was what she had to say. "Why can't you just accept that you're a...visitor here." I shot her a quick glance. I think she had almost said, "tourist."

"There must be something I can do that these people can't," I grumbled.

"How about Italian cooking? Water-skiing? Didn't you used to be a yo-yo champion when you were twelve?"

"Give me a break."

She looked at me for a minute, I thought sympathetically.

"Well, there is one thing," she said.

"What?"

"I'll give you a hint. We're doing it right now."

Once in a great while someone did ask me something about the English language. Teresa, the teenage daughter of Remedio of the grocery, once shyly approached me in the shop and asked, "Alturo, what does *dongo* mean?"

"Dongo? That's probably a country in Africa."

Puzzlement clouded her pretty, stolid face.

"No, Alturo. *Ingles.*"

. I knew the pupils of her age were studying English as part of their secondary school requirements, but I had never heard any from them except the "hey-lo!" greeting of younger kids. This was my first challenge as an interpreter. I shrugged.

"What about *wei*?" she asked doggedly.

"Well, that depends. "Weigh" means *pesar*, like when your mother puts sausages on the scale. Or it could be "way," which means either a direction or a manner of doing things. Or, maybe, like lifting a ship's anchor from the water..." I let my voice trail off as bafflement and despair returned to her face. "Why do you want to know?"

"Nothing," she said. "It's just in a song on the radio."

"What is? What does it say?"

"Something like '*dongo wei.*'"

"That's not English," I said. "Are you sure it's not French or something?"

Teresa expelled her breath in frustration. "It's *los blues,* Alturo. *Americano.*" Her manner told me that I was not only too past it to listen to the radio, but that she doubted that I could really speak English at all. It turned out that she was acting as a delegate of a group of teenage music lovers. The schools couldn't raise much interest in these kids to address academic subjects, but the power of pop music could.

"I tell you what, Teresa," I said. "I'll look it up and let you know." She didn't look convinced. Neither was I.

That night I tuned the radio to the Berja station the kids all listened to. We were in the sticks, but the DJ had the same egregious AM patter you will hear anywhere in the world. About half the pieces were in English, a jumble of old Beatles tunes, country western, rhythm and blues and schmaltzy ballads. I recognised some of it. Ellen looked at me over her glasses but said nothing. A blues song had me tapping my foot: "*Baby, pleeeeeze don' go.*"

I did a two count, then slapped my forehead. "*Dongo wei,*" I told Ellen.

"Of course not," she should have said, but she didn't.

That tore it. I was going to teach English to the pupils of Cantilla. Not only would they learn to understand the foreign

146

radio anthems of their adolescence, they would get the best possible grades on their exams. I might not be much good around horses, and might be pretty stupid about irrigation, but one thing I did know, by God. English! I tried to interest Ellen in the project, with no luck. She was beginning to complain that I was treating Cantilla like a Third World assignment, instead of a temporary retreat. I ignored her negativity.

The mayor wasn't convinced about us. I was a *buena persona*, but he wasn't, or at least that's what everyone said. He was known as *El Bicho*, "the bug." After consultations with both Pacos and a few other people, he agreed to let me use an upstairs room in the old *ayuntamiento* on Wednesday evenings for my English class. He came around to the house one evening, looked dismissively at our alien renovations and asked a few questions. Where were we from? Why did we want to teach English? Were we going to charge for our services? It sounded like a job interview but felt like an interrogation. It occurred to me that he might be fishing for a bribe. I smiled sweetly, but Ellen kept a frown on her face until El Bicho finally left.

My first class had six students. Teresa, a boy with terminal acne that followed her around like Mary's lamb, a pair of twin sisters who spoke to each other exclusively, an earnest-faced short guy that looked too old for secondary school, and Tonio, overweight son of Guisado, who showed surprisingly little defensiveness about his pariah father. All six were there when I climbed the creaking stairs of the *ayuntamiento* into a room that held five rusting typewriters from a failed government education scheme from seasons past. They were sitting randomly around an ornate teacher's desk. I was carrying a stack of materials from a short course in English teaching I had done several years before in England, including a telescopic metal pointer in the vain hope there might be a blackboard. I knew just what to do, however.

147

"Hello!" I greeted them, and put my hand behind my ear.

There was no response. I said it again, louder, "Hel-LO!"

There was a tentative murmur from Teresa and a giggle from the twins. I pressed on, "My name is Arturo." This accompanied by a gesture, practised in the hall mirror, of touching myself on the top shirt button. "What's your name?" I pointed at Teresa, who looked startled for a moment before answering, "Alturo."

"No, listen," I said in Spanish, already breaking my resolve to do the whole class in English. "MY name is Arturo, your name is Teresa." She nodded warily. Tonio and the old-looking teenager exchanged glances.

"Let's try it again. My name is Arturo. What's your name?"

"My name is Alturo," said Teresa.

"No, no. MY name is Arturo," I repeated.

"MY name is Alturo," said Teresa obligingly. I looked at Tonio hopefully.

"My name is Alturo," he said.

They had brought their school textbooks. They sat stoically while I browsed a dog-eared chapter of Teresa's book. It was brightly illustrated with photographs of a group of youthful holiday-makers in front of a London double-decker bus. Behind them could be seen the face of Big Ben hanging unrealistically overhead. The models looked stylish and unlikely. There was one black man, an oriental woman, a handsome chap in a Liverpool football jersey and a blonde with trendy streaks of green in her hair. Just what the kids of this pueblo in the back of beyond needed to identify with. The chapter was about telling time. The photo of Big Ben said it was ten minutes past ten. The black guy was pictured looking at his wristwatch. Below the picture were sets of questions and answers about the hour, set against pictures of watches and clocks of all kinds. *What time is it? It's ten past ten,* said the caption.

"What time is it?" I asked suddenly. To my amazement, all six of them chimed in, "It's ten past ten." Clearly they had been drilled at school. Cunningly, I looked at my wristwatch and swivelled my arm so that all could see.

"What time is it?" I asked, smiling encouragingly.

"Ten past ten," said Tonio and one of the twins in unison.

"No," I said patiently, "What time is it *now*?"

There was silence. I pointed to my watch again. "Ten past ten," said all six.

I shook my head. "Look. Little hand on eight." I held up eight fingers. "Big hand on nine." Flashing five then four fingers. "What time is it now?"

Brows furrowed. Weight shifted in chairs. Tonio looked at Teresa, who was biting her lip. I held my arm in the air, touching the dial of my wristwatch, a crooked grin of encouragement fixed on my face. It was the old-looking kid that broke the silence.

"Ten past ten," he said.

It was Teresa who rescued me. She reached under her chair and brought out a portable radio/cassette player and put it on the desk. For a moment I thought she had brought English language learning tapes, and that we could all listen to someone else struggle with teaching. Cassettes materialised from all six of them. They sat in front of me like offerings on an altar. I looked at Teresa. She smiled, held up a cassette and said, "Billy Joel."

There will be someone, I'm sure, who could explain to six adolescents who had never been further than Ugijar what an "uptown girl" is. In a place where there is no uptown, no downtown, no town at all, translating English songs into Spanish is a high calling. Unfortunately, this wasn't covered in my short course in Canterbury. I didn't let that stop me, though. I was determined to make a go of this class, one way or the other. Realising that by the time they had enough fluency

149

to unmask my lies I would be long dead, I began to let my imagination flow. I told a story of a girl whose parents didn't approve of the singer, who had to go to great lengths to be with his love. I poured it on a bit when I saw their interest. I embellished it even further, and before I knew it I had a classic tale that borrowed heavily from the Bard. The students were rapt. I enjoyed myself, too. When Ellen asked me how the first class had gone, I was able to tell her, without lying, "Great."

The classes took on a predictable form. I struggled for half an hour or so with introducing bits of English based on the schoolbook while the students sat patiently. Then we turned out attention to Abba, Wham and K.C. and the Sunshine Band. These all turned out to be storytellers of the first rank, producing gripping tales of heroic warriors, imprisoned princesses and evil sorcerers. The *ayuntamiento* became Ali Baba's cave. Enrolment swelled until we had to borrow chairs from Paco's bar. I got into the habit of dropping by after class to see him.

"The English class is going well, then," he said one night.

"Not too bad."

"And the young people—they are learning English?"

"Little by little," I said, wanting to change the subject.

"That's good," he said. "Their exams are next week."

The following Wednesday I went to the *ayuntamiento* loaded for bear. I was determined that the students would have at least some benefit from the weeks I had spent with them. There was no doubt that their appreciation for the language had grown. English pop music, a la Alturo, had opened a whole new world of myth and legend. They surely would want to be able to understand the words themselves. Good. By the time they did, I would be dead and gone and beyond exposure as a plagiarist.

The last lesson in the section of the course they were doing at school involved the contents of a lady's handbag. There were photographs of objects: a ballpoint pen, a mirror, a purse, a pair of glasses and a comb. These combined with verbs: take, put and carry. There were prepositions: into, out of, with, etc. Before the last class I borrowed all of these items from Ellen. I wanted reality, focus. I went through the plaza swinging my handbag without embarrassment. There were sixteen students waiting when I arrived. They would have dozens of cassettes ready for me. Okay, I thought, this is D-Day. Tonight, like it or not, we are going to learn some English.

Ellen and I had been speaking Spanish for so long now that we didn't have to think about it very much. If there was a word we didn't know that came up in conversation, we looked it up in the big dictionary when we got home. I was confident.

Far too confident.

I got them all around the desk and dumped the contents of the handbag onto the surface. Sweating and grim-faced, we went through the motions of putting and taking out, into, over and under things. Glasses, pen, purse. I asked each in turn what I was doing as I moved the objects about. Some of them got some right, especially Teresa, who was showing a real talent as a linguist.

The boy with acne, whose name was Pepe, was lagging behind. I focussed on him. He couldn't remember the English names of the objects, even though I had written the nouns in both languages on clearly visible cards. I helped by jogging his memory with the Spanish names: "Mirror. *Espejo,*" and pointing to the cards. He repeated what I said. I got to the comb, and he looked at me blankly. "Comb," I said slowly. *Peine.*"

There was a sudden intake of breath around the table. A tall kid I had grown to dislike sniggered. Puzzled, I repeated, "Comb. *Peine.*" This time the laughter spread around the room. I felt myself begin to blush. Looking around for a friendly face, I caught the eye of Teresa just as she exploded into laughter.

The whole room joined in. I realised I had made another of those gaffes for which I would be guaranteed years of frequent wincing. It was Tonio who intervened.

"No, Alturo. *Peine*. Pay-ee-nay. Not Pay-nay." He had assumed a helpful expression, but mirth was threatening to overwhelm him. I gave it a second, then realised that my accent had turned the innocent word for comb into the polite name for the male sex organ. *Peine*, not *pene*. Comb, not penis. Aware that this was a defining moment in my pedagogical career, I gave them all a sheepish grin and said, "Right. Pay-EE-nay! Thank you." The laughter subsided. I had come out of this okay. The teacher was not only a caring, *apanado* person, he was humble as well. No doubt this gaffe had given me extra respect. Now all that was needed was to push on, to get this lesson down pat. We would still triumph, just wait and see.

I turned to Teresa, my star pupil. I picked up the comb and slid it into the purse.

"What did I do with the comb?" I asked, adding carefully, "*peine*."

Maybe all teachers have moments like this one. For me it began as a gnawing sensation, a growing premonition of disaster that formed itself in my horrified mind just as Teresa was beginning to move her lips. In slow motion, like in the first moments of a car crash, I raised my hand to stop her, opened my lips to intervene, but it was too late. Looking carefully at the English word for *monedero*, she spoke in a clear, confident voice.

"You put it in the poor-sey," she said.

Chapter Eighteen

Winds

When winter came to Cantilla, I felt it. It wasn't just the cold that crept up the stairs and pursued you into bed, or the need for more and more trips to the river to get firewood. A chill had begun to settle on to Calle del Rio that had nothing to do with the weather.

Ellen and I had all but finished the house. With the end of the all-consuming project, the days got longer. Silences appeared that weren't comfortable. As Ellen ran out of urgent tasks, she tried to turn to her old resources of drawing and painting, but they weren't going well. I knew this because she rarely showed me what she had done. Sheets ripped from her sketchbook became a source of tinder for the fire.

I responded with artificial cheerfulness. I whistled and told jokes. I started sentences with phrases like, "Tell you what, why don't we…" It was as if I wanted to fill the silence so that hard questions couldn't pop up. Questions I dreaded, like when we might go to London, and when we might see family and friends. These would be bad enough without the big one: "Art, what are we actually doing here?"

Christmas came and passed pleasantly enough. Bill brought his girlfriend, Raquel, from Madrid and we rigged a metal oven to cook a goose he had brought all the way from Granada. Raquel was fascinated. We were the first Americans she had met that were living the rural life in Spain. I regaled her with Third World stories, and Ellen filled in the biographical details. Bill, whose life had been spent serenely contemplating the world, just smiled. I could always rely on him. He never questioned our idyll in Cantilla, or asked how long it would last. For a few days our lives seemed as I had imagined them.

A few days into January, Ellen got a letter from an old friend, Peggy Seeger, a well-known folk singer, baby sister to Pete. Ellen had played a few gigs with her when we were in London. I got along well with her husband, Ewan McColl, the firebrand political radical, director and singer. Peggy suggested that Ellen and I spend a few days in London. There was talk of starting a new all-female group. Ellen was excited, and I tried to be excited, too. The thing was, I didn't really want to go. I didn't need to tell her this, and neither of us wanted to reveal the split. So we held out until one afternoon, when Ellen got a fat envelope from the postman. It contained details of a course at the London branch of an American university. It would help lead to the completion of her degree left unfinished for years. It also meant that she had written to the university without mentioning it to me.

As always, Ellen had already thought things through. We would go together to London for a few weeks, where she could look into the course, which started the following autumn. She could work out a few songs with Peggy and another singer and they could try them out at the Red and Green Umbrella Club in Islington. I could... well, I could look for a course, too. Ewan and I could have a few beers while the women practised. We could get an inexpensive room at the London branch of our old sending agency from Botswana days. She was excited. I tried to look excited, too, but the silences returned.

We were sitting in front of the fire, baking potatoes and peppers in aluminium foil, our favourite way to cook. I fiddled with the dial of the short-wave radio. The signal was never reliable, and we still depended on the BBC World Service for our news. There was a Europe-wide cold wave, it seemed, that had paralysed rail services north of Watford. Ellen pretended she didn't hear.

Kamikaze that I was, I burst out with, "I can't believe you want to go up there and freeze your... get so cold."

"It's not about weather, Art," she said levelly.

"Well, what about the house?"

"What about it? It's been all right for two hundred years so far. It can probably survive a few weeks without us." She said something else under her breath.

"What?"

"I said, 'so can Cantilla.'"

"I don't want to go. Not yet."

She put her book in her lap. "Art," she said in a voice that I could tell needed a lot of control, "We can't just sit around here forever."

"Who's just sitting around? I'm not sitting around. I've never been so busy in my life." I stood up, as if for emphasis. "Tell Paco or Francisco or even Guisado they're just sitting around, why don't you?"

155

"They're from here. It's the only life they know. They don't try to make a career out of enjoying the scenery. They're rural peasants, Art. You're not."

"But, Ellen, this place is...special. It's the most perfect place I've ever been. We can't just come and go, use the village like a...a vacation spot for British tourists."

"Why not?"

"What?"

"Why can't we use it as a place for vacations? It's cheap, it's friendly. We own the house. We're not obligated to spend every day working the land."

"No, but... I can't believe you're saying that. We're not tourists."

She paused. I thought her features softened, perhaps with pity.

"Then, what are we?" she said.

If I ever allowed myself to think about Ellen's last question, I suppose I would have said, "I'm a pilgrim." I would mean that, whereas it was possible to see our peregrinations between countries as drifting, I had the vague idea that I was looking for something. If I had been honest with myself I would have seen that Ellen was different. She wanted purpose and order; if not a nine-to-five job and a house in the suburbs, at least a meaningful approach to such things as career and home. The future was with her in a way that my Peter Pan rationalising couldn't or wouldn't face. It didn't matter so much when we were working overseas, where just being among the local people was enough. There was enough definition in the activity to satisfy Ellen, and enough freedom to keep me happy. For the first time I wondered if Cantilla wasn't threatening to become a village too far.

We ate in silence that night. Neither of us wanted to say anything that would widen the rift that had begun to appear.

Two weeks later, Ellen left with Paco Taxista's morning run to Granada. We had agreed that she would fly to London, where she would stay at the agency's hostel and start investigating the course and the singing group. I would come after the fiesta in two weeks time. In the meantime, I would telephone her whenever I could. One of us, I argued, had to be there for this important event in Cantilla. But we were splitting up for the first time in years, and both of us felt it. The last few days we were inseparable, even holding hands when no one was watching us as we went up the trail to Bill's. When I heaved her bag into the boot of the taxi I had a lump the size of the cemetery rock in my throat. She cried a little, but as she got into the front seat I saw that look she had when faced with challenging events, a combination of determination and something like belligerence. I walked home quickly in the pre-dawn darkness and sat for a long time at the kitchen table.

The house was finished, or as finished as it would ever be. Furniture had gradually appeared, plastering and painting went on until one afternoon I found myself standing in the studio with paint on a brush and no place to apply it. The only remaining frontier was the corral, that vast, dark space at the rear of the ground floor where we had thrown everything we didn't know what else to do with. There was room for a workshop and a third bedroom. A window at the rear led onto a piece of vacant ground that I was told I could rent for a few pesetas a year from the church. All this seemed something for the uncertain future. So I just shut the heavy wooden door and ignored it.

I went up to Bill's and sulked. He had filled the rafters of the smaller house with bunches of *uvas del barco*, a variety of grape that didn't rot over the winter. They just dried up but stayed good to eat. I ate grapes and complained about the weather, which had turned cold and cloudy; prices; Guisado; the neighbour's son, who practised football goals against the front of my house; my bald left rear tire; my tendency to catch cold; the Tory government; my demonic cat and the dangerous curve on the highway. Bill ate grapes and made philosophical remarks. It was a satisfactory way to avoid complaining about Ellen's being a thousand miles away.

We took the car to Ugijar. I made up errands and so did Bill. I tried half-heartedly to make Paco El Chumbo smile, but my wintry mood had taken the edge off my sense of humour. One day we were on our third round of *tapas* in Chumbo's bar when Roberto came in, two middle-aged English women in tow. They were wearing backpacks and woolly bobble hats and gushing about the charm of Ugijar. Bill's back stiffened when he saw Roberto and mumbled under his breath that it was time to leave. But Roberto had seen us and led the two women over to our perch at the bar.

"Hey, look who's here. The pioneers of Cantilla," he said brightly.

"How things going up there?"

"About the same," I said.

"I told these two," he said to the women, pointing to me, "I told them not to try to get a place on their own, like. So they wound up getting a bad deal. Didn't I? Didn't I tell you?"

"No."

"Well, ladies, let these two be a lesson to you," he laughed. "No, just kidding." The women smiled and stood back in embarrassment at the tension in the situation. "These two ladies are seeing a place with me today. A *finca* up in Valor."

"Really?" I couldn't keep the sarcasm out of my voice even if I wanted to. Bill stared at something on the ceiling.

"A big piece of land and a house that only needs a little work," Roberto said, gesturing widely with his hands. "Has its own spring, too. A real bargain."

"That's great."

"Don't you just love it here?" one of the women asked. She had gingery hair and freckles and no makeup. She looked like a nice person. Too nice to be in Roberto's clutches. She looked at her friend. "We just can't believe the prices. And, my God, the scenery."

"How's your Spanish?" I asked her.

Her friend said, "I did a little in school. I think we can pick it up. Anyway, Roberto can do the translation for us." She smiled uncertainly. "Do you think it's really important?"

"Let me put it this way," I said, feeling like somebody telling a child there is no Easter Bunny, "If you don't speak Spanish, you won't be able to stay." Her face fell. I could feel Bill squirming beside me.

"You'll speak it in a month," said Roberto, frowning at me. "It's no big deal."

"If you don't speak it, you have to rely on friends," I went on, unable or unwilling to put the cork in. "And those are hard to find." I kept a steely gaze on Roberto, whose face darkened.

"Let's get moving, ladies," he said. "Arturo, the expert, has only been here, what, six months?" He steered them toward the door. The ginger-haired one raised her eyebrows. I shook my head. Roberto's face was hard. I realised that he could be more than a nuisance. I turned back to the bar, feeling empty.

"If you're finished ruining peoples' day, Art, we could go back home and drown some kittens," Bill said.

We didn't have much to say on the way home. I drove a little too fast. When I dropped Bill at his drive, I said, through the window, "I'm not going to let that guy screw this place up."

"Right. It's your paradise, isn't it?" he said over his shoulder.

That night the wind started. It woke me out of a doze on the couch. At first I thought it was the howling of the demon cat, a high pitched keening noise like nightmares of banshees and creatures straight out of J.R.R. Tolkien. It rose and fell with each gust. I went looking for the source of the sound and found the shutter in the upstairs bedroom bulging against its latch. I stuffed a pillowcase in the crack and the keening stopped. I went onto the roof and looked up the valley. Clouds were racing down the Sierra flashing like signal flags in the dim glow above the village. Antennas and clotheslines were rattling metallically, threatening to leave their moorings. Scraps of discarded paper and plastic bags whipped around in small whirlpool patterns from the street. The wind was cold, not chilly, but bitter cold that cut clean through your clothing. I secured the hatch, watching over my shoulder for the cat, and went downstairs and built a fire. I turned up the radio to drown out the sounds of the wind and maybe to drown my thoughts. Ellen's chair looked emptier than ever.

The wind blew for three days. People went along the streets bent at strange angles, their skirts and trouser cuffs whipping against their legs. Paco Junior wore a new hand-knitted cardigan. The bar had lost its air of warmth. You could see your breath as you stood waiting for *tapas*. Just a few people ventured out. I asked Paco if this wind was usual.

"People ask me that every year," he said. "We forget about it, but, yes, it happens all the time." I didn't respond.

"Aren't you going to ask me how long it usually lasts, Arturo?" he said.

"Okay, how long does it usually last?"

"I don't remember," he grinned.

Bill said it lasted a week last year. He was hunched over his butane stove, wearing a sheepskin coat as we ate honey on some bread I had brought from Latigos. We didn't mention the two women or Roberto.

It was the heart of January. The first almond flowers were appearing on the bare black branches of winter. Farmers were worried that the wind would take the blossoms. No blossoms, no almonds. Bill said that they had the same worries every year, but that there were still almonds all the same. His trees, located on a sheltered slope, were just at the budding stage. He wasn't worried.

Aparicio turned up on foot. The horse was in his corral. People didn't like to take their animals out in the wind because flying twigs could make them start on a tricky bit of trail. He had on seven layers of clothing, as he showed me. He looked like the cartoon man for Michelin tyres. He said the wind would blow itself out tonight. Bill didn't say anything, and I didn't ask Aparicio how he knew.

The following morning I was awakened by a shaft of sunlight through a crack in the curtains. Something was different, but I didn't know what. It was only when I opened the kitchen shutters that I realised the wind had stopped. The constant howls and whistles had been the background to my whole world for three days. Now, in its absence, I could hear the sounds that made Cantilla familiar: the clop of horses on their way to the fields, the idiot crowing of late-rising roosters, the bugle tones of a woman punctuating the slap of her washing on the stones of the fountain with the keen strains of *cante hondo*, lost love and death made beautiful by the return of the golden air.

I walked along the river, carrying an axe and a leather strap to collect the branches broken by the wind for firewood. I took some of last night's bread and a *chorizo* with me. Climbing the trail on the other side of the river, I kept going, charged by the brilliance of the day, until I reached the *secano*, or dry land, above the highest *acequia*. I sat on a rock in the middle of a field of almond trees whose branches had burst with pink flowers, thickly covering the hillside. Cantilla was stretched out before me like cherished possessions arrayed on a shelf. I could see, even at this distance, people I knew, going about their business in this new world that had emerged from the storm. I realised that I had emerged from something, too. Without being able to explain it, I felt that I owed the *pueblo* an apology.

Chapter Nineteen

Fire!

I never have found out why Cantilla has two fiestas every year. All pueblos in Spain, probably in the world, have one major festival honouring the patron saint or visitation of the Virgin that has a special relationship with the village. Cantilla's was in late summer. But Cantilla also had a winter fiesta at the end of January. True, statues of the Virgin were brought respectfully from storage and paraded through the village. There was a special mass, attended by the same black-dressed women who marched behind the Virgin singing hymns in a brassy harmony that sounded like strains of a concertina. But these somehow seemed like window dressing to justify something that had probably gone on since prehistory: a wild winter booze-up to strengthen the frost-weary soul.

You could tell fiesta was on its way. For a few workers it started four days early. Men stayed home from work. They did not shave, and could be found in both village bars at an early hour. Strange visitors turned up from Granada and Madrid. The glowering shepherds, flaunting their reputations for wildness and sexual excess, left their sheep in corrals and spent their days in the plaza. Other men avoided them. Rudolfo, Gregorio's grandson, in charge of fiesta fund-raising, collected from me twice. Once, shiny-faced on the Monday; the second time on Thursday, the day before things began, somewhat the worse for wear in his pre-festival celebrations. I didn't mind.

I didn't know what to expect. People had been talking about the fiesta for weeks, ever since the brief party that was Christmas in Cantilla had ended on the sixth of January. Christmas, and the Day of the Kings, when the children got their presents, had seemed a little perfunctory. The real party was going to get underway soon.

By Thursday night, the village had filled to capacity. Women were seen out in the evening sporting city clothes. Children who lived in the big cities carried flashing electronic toys and other status-bestowing items that the year round Cantilleros hadn't seen. Boys of twelve raced through the streets on motorbikes belonging to older cousins. For the first time in months I drew stares. The returnees from the cities hadn't seen a stranger in town before. I greeted everyone with the rough accent I was beginning to acquire in order to make myself understood. I wanted everyone to see that I was a *buena persona.*

The first bomb went off about seven on Friday morning, propelling me from bed with the adrenaline-born alertness of someone in a war zone. Paquillo, the other mason, was standing at the railing at the bottom of town surrounded by boys. He lit skyrockets with casual unconcern, touching the fuses to a cigarette dangling from his lower lip, putting the fire-spitting wooden handles in the pipes wired to the railing at exactly the last instant. In the gloom that still clung to the valley, flashes would etch the faces of the buildings, followed milliseconds later by booms that echoed up and down the valley as far as Cherin to the south and Bayarcal to the north. This was the intent, of course. Let it be known that Cantilla is in fiesta.

I stayed inside until I was sure the last of the morning's barrage had gone off. I had outgrown my love of explosions at an early age. During the whole long weekend I was to skulk about avoiding fireworks with only the trembling dogs for company. Cantilleros loved the bombs, and this year they had a bumper crop.

I got to the plaza about ten. To my surprise there were no parked vehicles to be seen, these having been cleared in the wee hours. Men were standing alongside their horses, mules and donkeys. Boys threaded excitedly between the clusters. Those older than twelve were carrying *botas*, goatskin bags used as wineskins. I saw Jose, Francisco's brother, sitting bare-backed on a mule. He grinned broadly at me and called one of the larger boys, a tall lad with a cowlick already called El Largo, "the long one." El Largo came over to me and said in a loud voice, "Eleven. Alturo, eleven!" He held the wineskin at shoulder level. Jose gestured with his finger at his open mouth. Filled with dread, I opened mine while El Largo projected a small but lethal stream of local wine into my throat. Boys surrounded him, chanting *"Uno, dos, tres..."* The stream of wine stopped at eleven. That was to become a dreaded word in the three days that followed. If I had arrived an hour later, I would have become, like the unfortunate in-law from El Ejido, in the village for the first time, number forty-three.

I hung back as far from the boys as possible, looking around for friends. Paco Taxista was nowhere to be seen. Paco Junior was in his bar. Guisado sat by himself on the wall. No one gave him a number. At a certain moment, arrived at without consultation but with total agreement, we left the plaza in a long, straggling procession, down the streets past my house, where for one moment I considered jumping ship, and out the stony road into the country side. Most men were mounted, but a few, like myself, mostly visitors, walked along behind. The boys, getting animated with their tasks, squirted jets of wine into the mouths of men on horseback, with variable results. The shirts and jackets of the riders were soaked before we got to the river. I asked Pedrillo, an older man I sometimes stood next to in the bar, where we were going. He just pointed across the river in the direction of the *rambla* and said, "To get *mata* (brushwood) for the fire."

We went up the sandy slope of the *rambla*. The horses were slipping on the steep incline. Men called to each other, joking obscenely in the absence of their wives, teasing each other about their horsemanship as the wine took effect. Next to me Pedrillo was puffing with exertion and I was sweating through my jumper. Near the top of the *rambla* El Largo caught me again, and I realised that if you closed the back of your throat you didn't have to swallow all the wine. This became an important bit of survival knowledge as the day progressed.

Most of us were drunk by the time we reached the dry land above the irrigation canal. Men got off their animals and sat on rocks while the boys gathered *mata*. These were pungent wild herbs, dried branches of rosemary and thyme. The growth from last summer broke easily in the hand. We made piles, and one by one the horses and mules were loaded with great heaps tied to saddles. I saw Francisco wobbling under a mountain of *mata*. He slipped and fell onto his backside with the load still on his head. There was a great laugh, followed by a long visit from the wine carrying boys. Francisco had lost his glasses. He was trying to explain, closing one eye elaborately, but no one was listening.

The mood had begun as jolly, but as the drunkenness increased, the atmosphere darkened. Two men had a brief fistfight, swinging useless roundhouse punches at each other while a circle of spectators jeered. A boy began to whip a reluctant mule with a leather strap. A few blows landed on the face of the animal, who was spinning in fear among a crowd of men. His uncle cuffed the boy to the side of the head, and he ran crying down the hill. It was already difficult to understand the rough Cantilla accent, but the drunkenness increased it became impossible. I was feeling it myself, and sat apart for a few moments to steady myself.

Some of us had already begun the trek home. I looked at my watch and realised that we had spent half a day up the hill. I joined the leavers, staying as far as possible from the boys, whose *botas* were emptying fast. When we reached my street I waved as heartily as I could and ducked inside. I caught a glimpse of myself in the hall mirror. I was covered with leaves and sticks. My sweater was wet to the waist with spilled wine. My head ached, and I was fighting off nausea. I showered and sat at the kitchen table. Francisco and Mari were shouting at each other in their kitchen across the street. The fiesta was half a day old and I was already praying for it to end.

The *mata* piled up in the centre of the empty square. While we had been on our drunken expedition, the women had begun the pile, heaping old chairs, bits of rotten rafters, mattresses, boxes of paper saved for months, straw unneeded for the now slaughtered pigs, and anything else that would burn. I arrived at dark, feeling better but anxious about what would happen next.

In the bar, Paco Junior was in high spirits. The *tapas* had been flowing all day. Men had changed their clothes, except for a few who reeled drunkenly through the crowd. The wine-carrying boys weren't allowed in the bar. It was like taking refuge in an embassy. I drank coffee and listened. The fire was to be lit at nine.

At five to, the artillery began again. Paquillo had been among the diehards on the *rambla*, and as the blasts shook the plaza, I imagined him reeling with a handful of smoking touch paper. There were at least three people I had met in Latigos and Cantilla who were missing fingers as a result of fiesta fireworks. I wondered if there would soon be four.

We spilled out into the plaza. Women lined the outsides. On every house balcony in the plaza, two women stood grimly with buckets of water at their sides. I couldn't imagine what this was for until two men poured five-gallon cans of petrol onto the margins of the pile, which had grown steadily through the afternoon. There were now old kitchen cabinets, a broken guitar and someone's legless sofa on top. Rudolfo, the de facto master of ceremonies, passed out torches made of sticks with petrol-soaked rags tied to the tops. With a great cry, taken up by everyone, of *"La Lumbre!"* the pyre was lit. Fire exploded into the plaza with a sound like wind through a tunnel. The heat was instantaneous; we were all driven back. Sparks and bits of burning cloth shot skyward like rockets. Air pockets in the middle of the fire exploded, sending clumps of flaming cinders near the buildings. My face burning, I pressed against a wall and watched as the grim-faced women on the balconies dashed water onto their shutters, to prevent blistering or even worse. The fire was making too much noise to hear voices, but the looks on faces said it all.. We were together in a situation of mad risk. The village could burn down, we could be injured or killed. We loved it.

The fire settled into a huge glowing furnace. The heat was still intense, and everyone had shed their outer clothing. The women on the balconies, casting one last suspicious glance at the fire, went inside. The heat pulsed in waves as material near its centre caught fire. The boys began their rounds again, but they were more subdued. I took my eleven count cleanly, leaning forward to avoid the spills. Amazingly, none of the boys seemed to have touched a drop themselves. That would come soon enough.

Someone pulled at my sleeve. It was Jose, Francisco's brother. He was pointing excitedly overhead. Necks were craning, eyes fixed on the roof of the former town hall, now temporarily to become a dance hall. On the roof, leaning unsteadily over the parapet, was a man I recognised as Manolito, one of the village's candidates for town drunk. He was a short, wiry man of thirty with a pair of thick black-rimmed glasses. He was naked from the waist up. In one hand he waved a huge plastic bottle of wine, a jeroboam down now to the dregs. The crowd shouted at him. He shouted back, unintelligibly. At the best of times he could hardly be understood. Some of the men were laughing, but I sensed a serious note underneath.

I had met Manolito one evening before Ellen went to London. The door of our house was pounded continuously for five minutes as I rose, shaken, from my bed and hurriedly dressed. Fearing some emergency—people came to get you if there was an urgent phone call at the grocery—I ran downstairs and flung open the door. It was Manolito, dirty from sleeping in some corral, clutching a soiled piece of paper in his hand. He was crying. Tears streamed down his face as he gabbled in a Spanish incomprehensible from the thickness of his accent and the wine he had obviously drunk. I let him into the foyer. Ellen peered down the stairs and I waved her away. Manolito thrust the paper at me with a hand black with grime. I took it between two fingers. He was repeating a phrase more or less constantly and making circular gestures with his hand that I took to indicate writing. I held the paper to the light of the shower room and tried to read.

It was a letter, a torn aerogram of thin blue paper. The writing was that of a woman. It appeared to have been written with a fountain pen. It began, "Dear Manolo," but it only took a few lines to see that it really should have said, "Dear John." I looked at the signature, a curlicued squiggle that I nonetheless could make out as Rosario. I said, "Rosario?" and Manolito burst into a fresh gust of tears. He leaned against me. I pulled back, but out of sympathy tried to conceal the fact that his smell was overwhelming me.

"*Rosario,*" he snuffled, "*Mi Rosario.*"

The letter was a brief kiss off. Apparently Manolito had been corresponding with this woman for a while. The return address and the stamps indicated that she was in Cuba. It didn't occur to me to ask Manolito at that time how he had managed a correspondence, since he was clearly unable to read and write. In a surge of reckless pity, I invited him up to the kitchen. He straddled a chair and put his head on his folded arms and wept. Ellen stayed in the living room, but watched from a crack in the door. I shot her a defiant look and asked Manolito if he wanted a cup of coffee. He shook his head, violently, making the same clumsy circular motion with his wrist. "Write. Write a letter," he said.

I later learned that one of Manolito's contemporaries had sent away for a list of pen pals in some international youth magazine, giving his name as Manolito. He had claimed to be a large landowner, widowed at an early age, who wished to begin life again with a new partner. Rosario had responded with enthusiasm. One day, Manolito, who had never before had the postman call at his house, got a scented letter from Cuba, containing three pages of promising suggestions and a photograph of a thin woman with heavy eyebrows. It was a miracle. He carried the letter with him to the bars and had people read and re-read it aloud until its creases were torn. The photograph had not survived his continual caresses and had disintegrated. He talked a friend into writing a response, a florid declaration of Andalucian love and an offer of marriage. There was a good deal of merriment behind his back, but Manolito, accustomed to his life of more or less continual teasing, didn't notice.

Rosario's next letter came promptly. She was slightly concerned that his handwriting had changed since the first letter. She was cooler, but still interested. She asked for details of his farm and livestock. Yet another friend was found to respond on his behalf, but this time the writer was less concerned with decorum. In between Manolito's honourable declarations of love, he had interspersed fairly crude sexual suggestions. After waiting more than six months, tonight's letter, a spiteful rejoinder, had finally come.

I got most of the story from Manolito that night, and by nearly sunup had managed to put together a reply. In it, at his request, I pleaded for one more chance for Manolito to prove himself. I read it to him slowly, and he embraced me at the door. Ellen knew better than to complain when I was on a moral mission, and hardly mentioned my hurried shower at two a.m. It was Paco Taxista who filled in the blanks for me.

"That's cruel," I said. "Those guys are bastards."

He looked philosophical. "Arturo, haven't you ever noticed how the runt of the litter gets picked on by all the stronger ones? Dogs, cats, chickens, it's all the same." He shrugged. "That's natural. The other boys of his age have always picked on Manolito, but no one really wishes him any harm..."

"With friends like that..."

"...because he's one of us, you see. He's part of the pueblo."

I wasn't convinced. Manolito led a hard life. Because of poor vision, he had not learned to read. Because of a father who was gone a lot and a mother who spent her affections on a pair of Manolito's sisters, he had been a case of what people in North Carolina would call "hind tit." He learned all there was to know about horses and farming. He was known as a good honest worker when he wasn't drunk. Sober, he was shy to the point of discomfort. Drunk, he raved and cried, borrowed money, got banned from the bars and slept rough. His parents had begun when he was young locking him out of the house, so that he slept "*a la paja*", in the barn. These days he had taken up more or less permanent residence among the horses. He received a small state benefit, owing to his vision, but this, by the time it arrived, was already owed.

In the bars, Manolito would be treated with what seemed to me to be amused tolerance by his peers, most of whom were now married and employed in the greenhouses. His drunken speech would be the object of imitation, and he would be the brunt of occasional pranks. This did represent a form of acceptance, as if to say, yes, he's a living joke, but he's our living joke.

A day before the fiesta, following a period of months of abstinence, Manolito had crept up behind a van delivering wine for the celebration. He had grabbed a jeroboam of strong wine and made off with it. The wine salesman went for him in his corral, but there was no sign of him there. The general consensus was that he had gone to ground at his *cortijo* across the river, and that he would reappear when the wine was finished.

And so he had. He drained the last drops from the plastic bottle, and with the crowd calling his name, threw it onto the fire. He shouted something in what may have been a language of his own. Someone sent for his father. He was weaving dangerously near the edge three stories up. Like everybody else, I half hid my eyes from what I feared would be a tragedy. He pulled back from the edge suddenly and then appeared, running along the parapet wall. He leapt across the narrow street onto the roof of the building that held the Plaza Bar. He was lit dramatically by the flames as he soared, shoeless and shirtless, and disappeared onto the roof. The crowd moaned. A few men grabbed flashlights and ran along the building's side to the back, which bordered on a garden.

He was spotted, arms spread like a shaman in trance. The crowd packed into the narrow street. Voices pleaded with him to come down. Manolito shouted something that even I could hear contained the word *"adios."* With an expression somewhere between a benevolent smile and a grimace of pain, he executed an imperfect swan dive from the roof and disappeared into the darkness.

There was a collective expulsion of held breath from the crowd. A woman screamed. A dozen men, taking responsibility, surged forward. Some of them climbed a wall and disappeared into the garden. The rest of us froze. The fire was forgotten, fiesta forgotten, small cruelties and jokes recalled. I was torn between concern for Manolito and a cowardly desire not to see gore. I felt frozen in place. There was a hush, punctuated only by the crackling of the fire at our backs.

A head appeared over the wall. It was one of the men acting as rescuers. He waggled his finger, windshield wiper style. I couldn't tell whether he meant that there was no hope or no problem. He vanished again, and another head appeared. This was Manolito, missing his glasses, but plainly alive. He was covered with a fresh coat of what seemed to be horse manure. He was grinning, almost able to stand by himself as the men reappeared to hold him up. He made another indecipherable statement, maybe a revelation brought back from a near death experience, or perhaps just a request for a drink, and fell backwards into the arms of his rescuers, sound asleep. He was carried into the plaza and laid, snoring loudly, on the steps of the town hall. He bore a few scratches, but these could have been old wounds. No other mark could be found of his ordeal. Someone propped him in a seated position beside the door. No one wanted to get very close because of the aroma of the manure pile into which he had dived. He spent the rest of the night in that position, like a piece of garden statuary, until his father covered him with a horse blanket just before dawn.

Chapter Twenty

The Donkey in Day-Glo Socks

Nowadays not everyone in Spain has a *pueblo*. The migration to the cities over the past century has marooned several generations in urban bustle and alienation. But nearly everyone can recall a few days in summer when a visit was made to some small place in Andalucía, Cantabria or Cataluña in the company of relatives that talked funny, ate well and had no TV. This contact with one's origins is still very strong, perhaps even stronger now that the streets of Madrid and Oviedo have become indistinguishable from the streets of Munich or Edinburgh, the haunt of crack dealers, sex shops and sudden violent death for a few.

You could easily spot the people who had lived away for many years, or in the case of the young, who were born outside Cantilla. They spoke in accents that were more intelligible to my ears, wore clothing that was more linked to style than function, and seemed, with the exception of the children, to exhibit a reserve unfamiliar in the village, born of the caution of cities. In some ways they seemed to have more in common with me than with their equivalents in the pueblo. They appeared to approach the fiesta with the reverence of strangers witnessing charming but outdated custom, granting a kind of moral superiority to the sturdy women who still washed clothing at a fountain rather than in a laundrette, and to men who rode horses, not as a charming weekend pastime, but as a means of transport. The boys began within hours to imitate the rough tones of the Alpujarran accent and to mimic the behaviour of men who spat freely and seemed not to fear hard trails and large animals. Girls were closeted with grandmothers who cooked on fires and cheerfully broke the necks of rabbits for the pot. Men, exchanging pleated trousers for stiff new blue jeans, hid their soft hands in their pockets. Women fussed anxiously in kitchens, trying to show that they were still useful as well as ornamental. They had made a transition in a single generation from the middle ages to the middle class, and the pueblo brought this home to them.

If you have a conversation with a taxi driver in, say, Burgos, he will happily exchange stories of village life. It may be that his accent will coarsen as he speaks of olive trees and pig slaughters. Nostalgia for the village is very strong, a longing for an imagined innocent world left behind by a reckless century. Despite Spain's emerging influence, its innovative architecture, liberal lifestyle and burgeoning artistic accomplishments, it is possible to understand why Gandhi, speaking of India, called it "A nation of a million villages." If a Spaniard doesn't have a *pueblo*, he longs for one.

176

On Saturday the plaza had been cleaned of the remains of the fire. The young men who were the sponsors of the fiesta, those about to leave for "*la mili*," the compulsory year of national service, had stayed late and arisen early. Rows of streamers, provided by Alhambra Breweries, now flapped on strings hung from second storey balconies. A stage was being erected in one corner. There was no sign of Manolito.

By midday, folding chairs and tables had turned the square into an unoccupied cabaret. A couple of sullen gypsy traders set up their stalls, selling junk novelties and *turron*. Men who the night before had been seen reeling with drink were today, with a few exceptions, freshly shaved and dressed. Without warning, the revel of men had become the calm society of women. Family groups clustered together at the fronts of houses. Smells of the festive meals under preparation billowed through curtains. The talk was calm, interspersed with indulgent attention to children. The task of reuniting the village had begun with a thousand subtle negotiations. I found myself at odds in this more placid Cantilla, having no grandchildren to admire or mother-in-law to placate, so I went up to Bill's.

There was a strange car in the drive, a rental Opel from Malaga. I shrugged off a feeling of foreboding. It was becoming obvious, even to me, that I was reluctant to admit outsiders to Cantilla, though I couldn't say why. Lately, in the bar, passing through the plaza, I had been approached by people wanting to sell houses to foreigners. They were envious of Francisco's good fortune. Nearly everybody had an extra house, left them by a deceased parent or abandoned by a family member who had moved to El Ejido. I didn't respond well to these approaches, although for the sake of staying a *buena persona*, I had visited a few, making sure the sellers knew I wasn't interested myself. There were plenty of bargains, houses with spectacular views, houses with small attached gardens, even a magnificent ruin of a *casa senorial,* complete with arched veranda, where the family of the feudal landlords used to live. Not liking myself very much for it, I had occasionally overstated the risk of foreign hippies to the young women of the village and the general peace and quiet that Cantilla enjoyed. This didn't seem to matter much to anybody but me.

Aparicio was there, trimming dead branches from the grapevine that shaded Bill's patio. A middle-aged man and younger woman sat with pale faces turned reverently toward the sun. Bill was putting cups of tea on a low table. The traitorous dogs lay sprawled at the strangers' feet. They stirred when I came into view with a few half-hearted barks. I composed my features and joined them. Bill gave me a quizzical look, which I ignored. Aparicio grinned and said, "Arturo, the king of Cantilla."

They were Richard and Susan. They were from Bristol. They had been touring the Alpujarras. When they had braved a quick walk through Latigos, people assumed that they were looking for Bill, and had directed them here. They had fallen in love with Latigos, with the scenery and the lovely people. They couldn't believe the almond blossoms. Aparicio had been so kind. Richard could take early retirement in two years, and they had always had a dream of a little place in southern Spain.

To my credit, I didn't scowl. I nodded, and ignored a raised eyebrow from Bill as he served me tea.

"Don't you just love it here?" Susan asked. She was a pretty pale blonde with a blue bandanna on her head.

"When it's like this I do," I said, trying to keep my voice neutral. "Last week I might not have said so."

"We had some bad weather," Bill said abruptly.

Richard chuckled. "You should have been in Bristol. Our front garden was three inches under water." He was fit looking, balding pleasantly, wearing a blue chambray shirt. An expensive looking camera case hung from his neck.

178

Aparicio said something to Bill. To my surprise, Susan responded, in heavily accented Castilian Spanish. She and Aparicio laughed, and Richard joined in.

"You speak Spanish, then," I said.

"I try," she said, with what I thought was unnecessary modesty. "I did an A level at school and just sort of kept it up. We used to spend time in Barcelona whenever we could."

"I understand your village is having its festival," Richard said. "What's it called?"

"Cantilla. Yes."

"Oh, we'd love to see what that's like," said Susan. "Wouldn't we, Richard?"

"Do you think that would be all right?" Richard asked shyly. "I mean strangers and all that?"

I had reached a moment of truth. I hesitated, avoiding Bill's eyes. The selfish demon in me was screaming, "Say no. Just say no." No to people who fell in love with charming villages. No to fish and chips shops and pretty postcards of the plaza. No to well-heeled white bread ladies with Spanish A-levels. No to sharing my little lost paradise with other people. No to people, God bless them, that were not so different from Ellen and me.

"Sure," I said. "No problem."

The procession began at six o'clock, just as dark was filling the streets. There was one of Paquillo's bombardments that made me clap my hands over my ears even inside the house. It was a brief but furious episode like World War II carpet bombing. It stopped abruptly, and after a respectful silence, I could hear the sound of singing.

A mixed crowd of people, mostly women, were descending the hill, surrounding the statue of the Virgin carried by six proud, sweating young men. A school band from Ugijar, followed, playing on key but out of time with the bass

179

drummer. Then the women, at least a hundred of them, many carrying lanterns, swayed along in synch with the ponderous side-to-side oscillations of the Virgin's palanquin. Children were held in check in formations like human paper dolls, hand in hand. Most of them wore white shirts and blouses, in counterpoint to the black of their mothers. A few men, the alternate pallbearers, some pensioners moving slowly along at the rear, and the unmissable figure of Guisado, jockeying for a position of importance. There was no sign of the priest, who would be waiting at the church to perform the mass.

They came past my house, squeezing between the buildings, and just managing to turn the Virgin around the corner. Francisco, leaning from his kitchen window, removed a hat he had just donned especially for the sake of the gesture. I looked as reverential as possible, although no one looked my way. The parade passed quickly by, but I could still hear their brass-like voices for a long time.

After they had passed, I felt something like a chill. It wasn't the weather, or even the effects of yesterday's overindulgence. Images of the women in their black dresses, the familiar faces I saw every day, now transformed into something less familiar by the light of lanterns and the hypnotic solemnity of the procession. The Virgin, seen from behind, could have been any effigy at all, even one of the ancient stone figures thought to be fertility goddesses left by the prehistoric Iberians. It occurred to me that this thing would have been done, in similar ways, long before the Catholics attempted to stamp their ruling myths on it, before the Moors, and even before the Romans. There was something about the way the women's eyes had looked in the stark light of the lamps, as if they knew that what was being carried on here had to do with a female presence that had outlived civilisations that came and went in seasons and aeons. The mildness of the Virgin was somehow changed as she went her way through the streets into something strong, something eternal, and, yes, something dark. I brushed my thoughts away. Tonight was a time for fiesta, not philosophy.

It was a perfect opportunity to call Ellen from Remedio's grocery, as the women normally dragging their heels in the phone queue would all be parading. I climbed the hill and parted the bead curtain to find only Concha, the eldest daughter dandling someone's baby on her lap.

Ellen was home at this early hour. Leaning against a rack of potato chips, I shouted down the line. For some reason you always had to shout when phoning from Cantilla, because the psychological, if not the telephonic distance seemed so great. She wanted to know all about the fiesta. I told her about the two English people who were looking for a house. Wanting praise for my spontaneous act of generosity in allowing them to attend our fiesta, I got a silence from the other end. I pressed on. They were nice, clean, idealistic tourists, basically, clearly unaware of the complexity of the village, and...

Ellen interrupted me. "We bought a house, Art," she said exasperatedly, "Not the whole village."

Stung, I went on. "You know as well as I do..." I started.

"Chill, Art," she said. "Just chill."

Which didn't help my mood as I climbed to the plaza. This was almost unrecognisable as the oil-stained car park I had come to know. The stage was fully erected, with mountains of amplifiers and speakers packing the surface. Coloured spots and strobe lights and a huge mirrored ball hung from its roof, obscuring the whole front of Paco Taxista's house. Gaping teenagers in new shirts hung around, their eyes following the members of the band as they tuned their instruments. These had on black trousers with silver stripes down the sides and white shirts with frilly fronts and red cummerbunds. The female vocalist, a recent blonde with waist-length hair, wobbled unsteadily in a sparkly evening dress and stiletto heels. A few men, claiming their folding chairs early, sat eyeing her speculatively over glasses of wine.

At the fountain I saw El Largo, the boy in charge of the lethal wineskins of yesterday's expedition up the *rambla*. He and a small knot of other boys were surrounding a small white donkey. I saw that they were tying something to its head, and as I approached, saw that it was a bowler hat, holes cut in the brim to accept its long ears. It had on a pair of striped pyjama bottoms with a convenient missing patch at the back, a blue serge jacket cut to accept its forelegs, and on its back hooves, resplendent in the party lights, a knee-length pair of lime green day-glo socks. The boys were working assiduously, as if decorating a Christmas tree.

I had heard horror stories of the primitive customs of Spanish villages, in which animals were mocked and mistreated. In one northern village, I had heard, a donkey was actually thrown from a tower to its death during a certain celebration. My stomach turned over. If Cantilleros got up to something like that, I would lose some of my idealism about them. And even if, as Ellen would agree, an adjustment in my enthusiasm was no bad idea, I didn't think I could watch anyone torture an animal.

I tapped El Largo on the shoulder. At twelve, he was nearly as tall as I was. He had a freckled face and a towering cowlick. I asked him what they were going to do with the donkey. He looked blank. I went on. Were they going to beat him or anything like that?

"Beat?" he asked, polite as possible to an adult, even a stranger. "Why?"

"I have heard that sometimes people are cruel to animals in some fiestas, that's all."

He gave the universal windshield wiper sign, accompanied by a click of the tongue. "This is my father's donkey, Alturo," he said. "He's to make us laugh. Like a what do you call it, a mascot."

"Okay, then," I said, feeling foolish. I felt his puzzled eyes following me all the way to Paco Junior's bar.

The dance, like almost everything else, started late. I had miscalculated my own wine capacity, so that when the plaza filled with people, dressed and oiled unrecognisably, I was already a little the worse for wear. The band started playing at an uncomfortable volume, so that conversation, difficult at any time, was impossible. The folding chairs filled immediately, and people stood in a great circle around the plaza, clumped thickly near the outside bar Paco Junior had helped the sponsors erect. The party mood needed no time to get started. There was no hesitation as everyone able to stand on their own got up to dance. Old couples who I scarcely knew ploughed through muscular *paso dobles* with beaming faces. They were made up heavily, and women I had never seen in anything but housecoats and bedroom slippers took on the form of ageing Aphrodites. There was a whiff of something like sensuality in the air.

I saw to my surprise that men danced together as readily as mixed couples. Paco Taxista did a few turns with Paco Junior, and no one was laughing. Someone tapped me on the shoulder. It was Francisco, and I saw with a flash of terrible insight that he wanted to dance with me. Throwing back the rest of my wine, I extended my left arm, and then realised that Spanish people did things backwards. The man, the leader, clasps his partner's hand with his right.

The *paso doble*, at least as done in Cantilla, consists of covering a lot of ground with shoes sliding briskly across the floor in an anti-clockwise direction. The leader has the advantage of being able to foresee the inevitable collisions with other couples. Moving backwards, as I was, I could feel the people I connected with being moved aside by my larger bulk. The whole thing felt like those bumper cars at a fairground that are made to collide with each other. Francisco kept a smile on his face, which didn't reach my shoulder. He could have bitten off my second shirt button without bending. I tried to get some grace into my movements, but I felt like a dancing bear. When the dance was over, Francisco bowed from the waist with no visible trace of irony. I did the same.

I was just wrapping my fingers around another glass of wine when someone else tapped me. I turned to see the grinning face of Paco Taxista, whose sense of the ridiculous I had already observed. This time I got my right hand out first, put my left on the healthy bulge of his midriff and took off into the crowd without hesitation. Midway through the tune, I felt the substantial belly begin to heave beneath my hand. I cracked up too, and we finished the dance almost weeping with laughter. He knew what momentous elements of indoctrination I was having to overcome, and like the prankster he was, had been unable to resist seeing me suffer.

In the next few hours I danced with a dozen men and women of the pueblo. I was getting the hang of it. The band never stopped, and neither did we. The music, a poor collection of covers of Spanish and English pop mixed with traditional favourites, began to sound glorious. The singer's dress glistened in the strobe lights fetchingly. I felt romantic. I was aware that I was talking too much but nobody seemed to mind, even when, inevitably, I lapsed into English. I was in this state of exultation when I caught my first glimpse of Lola.

Lola was a girl of the village, now in her late thirties. She had been blessed or cursed from birth with one of those faces that is just a few points off stunning beauty. Her prettiness was evident even when she was wearing work clothes and her hair was matted with dust and sweat. She was at that point of ripening into middle age when her peers swelled into indifferent dumpiness and donned housecoats and slippers like their mothers. Her figure had changed in a way that only emphasised her feminine attributes. She seemed always to wear a searching expression, as people with myopia sometimes do, as if she had once seen or dreamt of kindness and thereafter spent her days trying to find it again.

She had been taken advantage of from an early age. Rumours of assignations with boys outside dance halls in Ugijar had accompanied her into adulthood. She had married a little late for comfort, and when she became a wife, everyone was a little relieved. There is something disquieting about having a girl of such attractiveness loose in the village. Men, married for life, treated her with a trace of rudeness, as if to ward off their rebel feelings. Women watched her movements carefully and made daily reports to each other. If she was seen wearing a new dress, especially one that displayed her ripe figure, women kept track of their husbands and sons.

The man she finally married was called Jose. He was thought to be a good man but a weak one, with a fondness for wine. They moved into a house at the top of town and had two children in rapid succession, two girls with the same threatening good looks as their mother, but because one kept her blonde curls into her third year, rumours inevitably circulated about who the father might be. For several years they had been living in El Ejido, but had only just returned to Cantilla following an accident to Jose that had made him eligible for disability payments. He now spent his time looking after the children, while Lola went daily to work in the packing houses.

Because I hadn't met Lola before tonight, it was inevitable that she would turn that vulnerable, searching gaze on me. When she did, standing beside me at the bar, I felt a small jolt of attraction that had nothing to do with the wine. And, because I was also a married man, I must have given off that subtle air of censure and pretended indifference that she had grown so accustomed to throughout her life. We didn't exchange a word, but she turned away with a gentle lopsided smile that made me want to apologise and, perhaps, put my arm around her fine-boned but sturdy shoulders.

In a place like Cantilla, sex and flirtation is reserved for the young. Even then, it is confined to the indulgence of the population toward the courting behaviour of the teenagers that took the form of nightly strolls up the road. There were dances at schools, and recently a disco had opened in Ugijar. The hormonal swamp of late adolescence was no less obvious in Cantilla than in any other place, but, by mostly unspoken agreement, it was left to the margins of village life. The young women were pretty. It was tempting to follow them with your eyes as they walked through the village, as you might in a city, but something subtle, perhaps communicated by the eyes of the women, kept you from this.

I had read somewhere about the typical iron grillwork on the fronts of many of the older houses of the village. At first glance they might have appeared to be designed to prevent theft, but since burglary was all but unknown in Cantilla, they were stylistic remnants of a time when courting took place under the watchful eyes of *chaperonas*. The courting young man could speak to the girl of his longing only in the presence of a minder, and his ardour was assumed to be so strong that it might take iron bars to restrain him. He would stand in the street, oblivious to the catcalls of his contemporaries, while he made what way he could with her affections through the bars of a cage. Cantilleros want their swains to be passionate and strong, but they don't want them jumping the fences.

Somehow this treatment of sexuality in Cantilla didn't seem prudish. Both men and women used coarse language freely, and sexual humour was shared openly. It was true that sometimes men might arrive home well after the bus, having

186

had a few drinks in El Ejido, where bordellos advertised with large neon signs. This was never mentioned, and the ancient bitter wisdom of the women made no obvious fuss. In a place where farm openly animals mate, assisted by the smallest of children, there was no hiding sex.

By now I had come to see the village not so much as a collection of houses, but as a collection of people travelling together through history. It was as if the pueblo was a ship, not for travel through space, but through time. Shipmates have to get along. There can be no rivalries, born of sexual longing, that threaten to capsize the ship that carries them, no divorce, open adultery, murder or theft. The preservation of the balance of life outweighs everything, even the secret lusts of common humanity. This sense of the necessity for getting along dominates every aspect of behaviour. Enemies must conceal, if possible, their hatred. Competition for things like water and choice land must be reined in by general consensus. And girls like Lola, for reasons not of their making, had to be controlled.

The party was still in full swing when I realised it was over for me. My Spanish was deserting me as the wine flowed down. Everyone I met offered me a drink, which now began to spill down my shirt. I was full of song. As I left the plaza I sang, but no one heard because they were all singing too. I loved Cantilla. I loved Paco and Paco, and Lola...well. Guisado was a great guy. The crumbling stonework of the houses was a miracle of design; the beauty of it all made me want to weep. I even loved Richard and Susan, who had made a brief appearance in the plaza, had one careful drink of wine and left after taking a picture of the party. I hadn't seen the shepherd, Rafael, but I would have loved him, too. They were all fine people, just fine.

I passed the donkey in his fiesta costume. He had been briefly paraded through the plaza, to mild amusement. He now stood tethered in front of Remedio's store, sleeping on three legs. One Day-Glo sock was tucked behind his other leg. The hat had fallen away somewhere, but the pyjamas, only a bit soiled, were still intact. I loved him. In a burst of insight I saw that the donkey was dressed up to represent us, our beautiful, silly, drunken selves, the asses of history. I gave him a hug, and in that instant conceived a noble plan. I would buy this burro. It didn't matter what it cost, or what difficulties there may be in owning livestock. It didn't matter what Ellen would say. It was a token of my acceptance by the village. I stood hiccupping, with my arms around the beast, composing verses.

A small boy passed. I asked him to go find El Largo, and tell him that I was taking the donkey home with me, and that tomorrow we would arrange for his sale. The boy looked at me round-eyed, nodded and vanished. I untied the rope and gathered the little uneaten pile of hay from the pavement under my arm. I spoke gently to the donkey and started downhill with a fistful of his rope.

He wouldn't move. He stood regarding me calmly with all four hooves set to the pavement as if they had recently grown out of it. I remembered something I had read somewhere, that donkeys have a unique attribute. While other beings may have will power, donkeys have "won't power." The calm look he was giving me was as much as to say, if you want me to move, you'd better have something better than this in mind, because I'm staying.

I pulled on his rope as hard as I could. His hooves slid a little on the stones, but his attitude didn't change. I pulled once more and slipped, falling heavily onto one knee. Free of the rope, the donkey turned again toward the wall where he had been tied and closed his eyes with what I thought was cruel unconcern. I brushed myself off and went home. Tomorrow I would make the donkey in the day-glo socks my own. I really would.

Chapter Twenty-one

The Invasion of the Triffids

The pounding on the door was a cruel imitation of the pounding in my head. I covered both ears with cushions from the sofa on which I had sprawled, but it didn't go away. Knowing it would be something I'd probably regret, I pried open one eyelid to find the living room bathed in sunlight. I was fully dressed, including my shoes. The pounding on the door became more urgent. Someone was shouting "Alturo!"

I got to the kitchen window by steadying myself on the furniture. I eased open the shutter. Below me was the head of El Largo. His cowlick was unmistakable. I spoke before he could begin a fresh spate of door pounding, a hoarse grunt of greeting forced through dry lips. El Largo looked up at me.

"Alturo, my father says he doesn't want to sell his donkey."

At first these words were meaningless, as if I had regressed to elementary Spanish classes or suffered a brain injury. As I put them into order, images floated up like wreckage after a depth charge: "...father (the forbidding face of El Largo's workaholic farmer parent)....donkey (the malodorous embrace of the burro in iridescent knee socks... sell (my alcohol-driven project to become a stableman)..." I experienced what a friend of mine calls a "wince wave," the sudden and uninvited memory of something said or done whilst bewitched or intoxicated. It rattled my already creaky bones.

"Okay," I managed. "No problem. Thanks anyway."

I started to close the shutter. I wanted darkness. It was almost accomplished when El Largo said,

"Right, then. Could I have him back, please?"

You can do quite a lot with a hangover if the emergency is great enough. I poured a pan of water over my head and rinsed my mouth with green minty mouthwash and did not vomit. Phrases ran through my mind: "Why, I don't have the donkey. What makes you think I do?" and "Oh my God, I must have left him untied. What can I do to make it right?" And (gruffly): "It's not my job to look after your livestock, Boy." None of these would do. I had left the burro standing loose in the street. It had wandered away, and it was *all my fault*. I threw the door open and just one look at my face told El largo all he needed to know.

"Let's go find him, then," he said, sighing.

On the rare occasions when a donkey is allowed out on his own, there are several predictable things he will do. He will find the choicest possible plants to nibble on, because, even though a donkey can thrive on the roughest of dry grass, he will, like all of us, go for luxury when it is available. In this case, the nearest thing to a donkey's dream was the flower bed of the cross old man who lived by the lower fountain. Then, having sated himself with delicious flower tops and the juicy leaves of newly sprouting onions, he will indulge his need to roll, to rid himself of the annoying ticks and gnat bites out of reach of his swinging tail. Finally, he may, if the occasion suits, enjoy a bit of running and bucking, especially if he is encumbered by anomalous gear such as pyjama bottoms and a blue serge jacket. Then he will do what donkeys like to do best: stand sleeping peacefully in the shade of an olive tree, with one day-glo sock tucked up behind him.

It is said that God protects idiots, babies and drunks. In this case he had done two out of three, because when we found the burro standing peacefully in Frasquito's garden, surrounded by the wreckage of carnations, zinnias and what would have been two sacks of onions, the owner was away tending his *finca*. El Largo took the rope firmly, made a clicking sound with his tongue, and led the donkey out of the garden and onto the road that wound down to the river. With a wisdom beyond his years, he put a finger to his lips, winked and started walking. The donkey's obedience offended me, but then I thought that perhaps the generations of farm animals had learned, as an important item of survival lore, to tell when someone was drunk.

"Oh, yes," said El Largo, turning back toward me, "My father invites you to his *cortijo*, down in the vega."

"When?"

"Today. We are going to kill a shoat." This delightedly, as if anyone in my condition would be all a-tremble at the thought of gore and infant mortality, Cantilla style.

"I'll be there," I said, not too grimly.

By two o'clock I was a little better. Still as papery as a patient recently released from hospital, I walked slowly down the rocky path to the river below my house, through terraces of late-blooming almond trees and the recently ploughed rows where onions and garlic were already sprouting beside the muscular new growth of broad beans. The sun was hanging lazily overhead, making it too warm for a jacket. People were in their gardens, hoeing and irrigating. As with all Sundays, the whole family was present. Men led mules and horses to tether at the edge of stone walls, women sat tranquilly with the youngest, while the boys and tomboys threw stones into the river and climbed trees. There were others there, too, visitors for the fiesta wearing their new blue jeans and rolled up sleeves.

At the river the land becomes flat. The river widens and shallows, weaving a twisted course through the meadows, forming little points of land bordered with round stones. The path, which ultimately leads to Cherin, crosses and re-crosses the river over well-placed flat stepping stones. A large projection of rock, rising almost to the height of the road above, dissects the *vegas*, forming two sets of fields. Downstream from where I was walking was an even larger area, reached by a narrow path from the highway nearly a mile downhill.

Antonio, the father of El Largo, had a *cortijo* built almost in the shade of the cliff. Like many farmers who had enough flat land, he only rarely went to work in the *invernaderos*. He could get two good crops of lettuce or Chinese cabbage a year from the wide terraces that formed his *finca*, as well as the large arbour in which he still grew table grapes for the market. And like many families who preferred being out in the countryside to being in town, the *cortijo* had gradually grown until it was as large as a house in the pueblo. Two storeys with a veranda, a separate barn and a balsa, or water tank, where children swam in summer. Because the family sometimes slept on the land, the *cortijo* had taken on the appearance of a home.

Antonio's wife, Consuelo, was wearing a blood-soaked apron as I neared the house. I was gratified to think that the shoat had at least, already met its end, and that I wouldn't be expected to help with the slaughter. The pink rivulets that had run in the streets during the *matanza* were all too fresh in my memory. Consuelo removed the apron and swept back her hair as I approached. She was a wide woman with bad teeth and that odd brass-coloured hair that comes from bottles in Remedio's grocery. Her smile was warm, and as she greeted me, she called Antonio from the stone barn.

Antonio was not a talkative man. He was taller than the average for the village, but his son had already outgrown him. Another son, Paco, only eight, also showed signs of unusual height. He appeared carrying a *pico mancage*, the all-purpose tool of the Cantillero farmer. El Largo was bent over a pit beside the veranda stacked high with freshly split firewood. He waved but continued his work. He was one of those Cantilleros, who even at his age, could make me feel foolish, and, given the events of the morning, now had proof.

Antonio's diffidence, I knew, was the result of painful shyness. He was one of the best farmers in the valley, perhaps because he preferred the lonely activity of the land to the chat of the bars. His handshake was strangely limp for a man of his obvious strength. With a kind of clumsy elegance, he dragged a straight-backed chair from the kitchen and gestured for me to sit. Consuelo handed me a bottle of beer from an ice cooler and a large plateful of olives. These were *caseras*, home made, with the splits caused when the fresh olives were struck with a mallet before being cured to speed the process. They had a sharp flavour that store-bought olives never had. I was gradually acquiring a taste for them that I knew couldn't be satisfied anywhere except in the rural villages.

I was the only one seated. I made conversation as well as I could, but soon realised that talk was surplus to requirements, and only caused the shy Antonio more embarrassment. The beer, really the last thing I wanted, seemed unusually cold and sweet. I sat as the fire in the pit was started, roaring at first with *mata*, then quickly resolved into olive wood coals that cast heat metres away. The sun was pleasant on my shoulders, and I began to feel less nervous. I watched the burro graze placidly, finally freed of his socks. Consuelo peeled potatoes from last year's harvest. A glimpse of the storeroom showed mountains of them lying dry and dark under rafters heavy with onions and garlic and dried peppers. The baby goat was oiled, wrapped in aluminium foil and buried in the glowing embers. It looked strangely intact, head and all. El Largo shovelled soil over the pit. Smoke oozed from the mound, and the aroma of cooking flesh mingled with the sharp smell of burning wood.

The family worked without speaking much. I got a sense of the rhythm of rural, really rural life, in which there is always something to do and someone to do it. I felt that I should be helping, but a glance from Consuelo showed me that, as a guest, I was already doing my part. The afternoon passed as these afternoons do, with reflected sunlight sparkling off the river onto a grove of poplar trees and the sound of gentle wind and flowing water. The scene was so perfect that it made me a little nervous. I was aware of the harsh realities of village life, of the hard resistance of the stones and the sharp stench of animal bedding, of the innumerable cuts and blisters of the working hands and the sad insufficiencies of life in a small place. I had had moments of something like despair along with these times of soul-expanding happiness, and I knew that nothing and nowhere was perfect, not even this. But at the same time I could almost hear my friends, Paco Taxista, tolerant and amused, Paco Junior, an answer for every occasion, Francisco's wry and fumbling eye for beauty, gently chiding me. *Don't think so much, Arturo. Just be here.*

The first chill of evening took me by surprise. The sun had long disappeared behind the rock cliff at our backs. Consuelo fried potatoes, onions and peppers in oil from the trees under which we were sitting, *papas a lo pobre*, to accompany the shoat. The family, responding to some inaudible cue, pulled chairs over to join me. A table that had no doubt seen much use as a slaughtering bench, was heaped with bread, dried tomatoes, slices of cured ham and raw onion. Antonio brought the shoat on a plank. The foil was covered in ash, but the meat inside was done to crackling perfection. We ate in silence. I felt the need to compliment the chef, or someone, but we all knew how good the meal was, and said little. I would learn, I told myself, how good it can be to be silent with others.

Afterwards, we sat back. El Largo, like his father, picked his teeth with a penknife. Consuelo unceremoniously dumped the used dishes and pots into a plastic tub. These would be done later, back in the village kitchen.

At last Antonio said, "It's a shame about the burro, Alturo. If I wanted to sell him, I'd sell him to you. He's for the woman," he said, nodding at Consuelo, who smiled.

I was surprised. He owed me a dressing down for letting the animal escape, and here he was, apologising to me.

"I could sell you that mule." He pointed with his knife to a large black animal at the edge of the arbour. "But I'd have to wait until we've got all the ploughing done. He's good, but he's getting on a bit. We need a new pair here."

This amount of conversation from Antonio was unusual. I felt flattered.

"I really don't need anything," I said. "Some day when I buy some land maybe. I was just a little, er, enthusiastic last night." I grinned sheepishly, but Antonio didn't respond. I guessed he never got enthusiastic like that. Out of kindness, it seemed, no one asked about Ellen. I wondered if people might be beginning to talk.

We drank coffee with goat's milk, and as the light began to fail, I stood up. They stood with me. We shook hands, and as I started back, El Largo joined me. He seemed to think I needed an escort. I didn't argue. We passed through their land around a bend, past some recently dug holes spaced widely on a flat unploughed field.

"Going to plant some trees?" I asked him.

"No, that's for the new *invernadero*," he said. We're going to put in a greenhouse." I stopped.

"What, one of those big plastic things? Here?" I was trying to control my voice.

"Yes," El Largo said, "A really big one. This whole terrace here."

"I thought it was too cold up here," I nearly whined. "They only work down at the coast, I was told."

"They've got a few near Ugijar now. Papa thinks he can get at least two crops of tomatoes and cucumbers. See, this *vega* is protected from the wind and it's got a lot of sun over here by the river."

I followed his pointing finger. I saw huge plastic blisters, their dried up sheets flapping in the wind, their stench of poison and artificial plant food and the dry ugly soil inside. I saw them creeping up the valley toward Cantilla like an invasion of Triffids, making the view from my roof terrace something to pull the shutters against, the *vega* a place to visit only under duress. Something in my reaction must have alerted El Largo. When he turned back toward home, he wore a blank expression that spoke volumes. Who could understand this foreigner?

As I walked home I tried to shrug off my feelings of encroaching disaster. I put myself in Antonio's shoes. He could make money with a greenhouse. He could even pay a few people to work for him once things got going. Fewer people would have to travel hard hours each day to work. And when the *vega* was full of greenhouses, no one would have to travel at all. Maybe someone would set up a packing house near the road, and the lorries would drive to Cantilla to collect the produce. The government would be forced to improve the roads. Land values would rise, people would move in. Cantilla would grow, like a smaller version of El Ejido. The dream of his fathers, to feed the family, make some money, build a new house of cement instead of stone and beams, would at last be possible.

What's the matter, Alturo? Got something against progress?

Chapter Twenty-two

London Fog

London was living up to its reputation. I took the late train from Gatwick Airport in a freezing downpour, gazing gloomily out the window at half-abandoned stations and lines of cars blurring reality with their headlamp glare in the rain-slick streets. At Victoria Station the queue for taxis looked like a crowd scene from *The Ten Commandments*. I pulled my thin jacket over my head and got on a night bus jammed with youthful revellers the worse for wear from a ten-pint night in the pubs. I felt out of place with my self-cut hair and my suntan.

Ellen was waiting in the foyer of the hostel. She hugged me with encouraging force and led me to a dining room where covered plates held my cold dinner of dry meat and two watery veg. While I ate, we sat talking in stage whispers because of nearby residents' bedrooms. She was paler but looked more energetic than I had seen her for some time. City life was clearly agreeing with her.

A folding bed had been erected in her room. It was a foot lower than hers, but I settled onto it with gratitude, propping up my head with my bag so that I could see her. On the walls were posters advertising venues where, presumably, she was performing. Her Martin D-Model guitar rested on the study table as if she had just been using it. I realised she probably had. A snapshot taken by Raquel over Christmas was stuck to the wall beside her pillow. It showed me clowning with Francisco and a scabby neighbourhood dog in front of our house. The sun was etching shadows on the walls, and I could see that we still needed another coat of paint on the door. I got up and lay down beside her, shoes and all, and put her head on my shoulder.

"Strange times, aren't they?" I muttered.

"Shhh," said Ellen, and we fell asleep.

We did what you do in a city like London when you haven't got much money. Ellen had regular hours running the check-in desk at night, so during the day we took in the galleries and walked in the parks. She was in charge here, arranging our activities as if I were a guest, which I suppose I was. She had always been a scourer of newspapers and magazines for bargains and special events. She kept *Time Out* under her arm everywhere we went. I followed placidly. The sights were interesting and even beautiful. From time to time, I managed to feel enthusiastic.

We got tickets to a West End play, arranged by Peggy and Ewan. I was surprised to find that I didn't look as out of place as I felt in my sink-washed Cantilla clothes. There were lots of students and shaggy sorts that managed to get hold of tickets. During the production, a drawing room tale of angst and alcoholism, I got fully involved. Ellen was rapt; her face was slick with tears of pleasure when we left. Sitting on the crowded Tube, we held hands.

It was as if she wanted me to see what it was about city life that attracted her. We had spent months together in London in years past, but this was somehow different. When she had come back for this extended visit, she was taking a new step into the unknown. She was hugging London the way I was hugging Cantilla. And whether or not a mere place can fill up what is missing inside, she was clearly engaging with London like a sinner takes to church: fervently. It was also clear that she had made a move from being my sidekick to having a life of her own. That stung. It was fair enough, but it stung.

The two weeks passed. I was noticing a small roll of extra flesh on my middle. I watched TV with residents from Sweden, Mauritius and China. They all seemed to like soap operas and Top of the Pops. I planted my flag in an armchair near the front of the lounge and took every opportunity to watch the worthiest programmes on BBC 2. If I was having a cultural experience in London, by God, I wanted to have one properly.

Aware that I ran the risk of annoying Ellen, I kept my mood level. I chatted with her friends, a plump refugee from Angola named Millie and a penniless Czech violinist whose name I can't remember. I was pleasant to everyone, knowing that I couldn't take my anxiety out on them. Or not very much, anyway.

On Ellen's day off we went out to the Kent suburbs to have dinner with Peggy and Ewan. They were as radical a pair as you can find on this side of prison walls. For years opposed to nuclear power plants, they had set out to foil the electric company in every way possible. Once they wrote out a perfectly legal cheque for their monthly bill on a six-foot plywood coffin. Another time it was a cake, done in icing letters. The company responded by installing a coin meter in their foyer. Every few hours one of them had to put a fifty-pence piece in the machine or the lights would go out.

They had their own folk music club, which changed venues every few weeks, in rented halls and the upstairs rooms of pubs. The crowd were a mixed bag of gothic punks and old-style revolutionaries who chain-smoked and spoke in gravelled voices. Hardly any of them had not been a guest of Her Majesty's government for a time, paying for their politics. I loved them. They made me feel like a middle-class weekend radical. But Ewan was kind to me. Despite his reputation as the fiercest stage director in London, he seemed to give me extra points because I had worked in Africa and the DR.

We sat in his living room while Peggy and Ellen sang in the kitchen. They were going to be called Jade, an all-woman folk group with attitude. Ewan had just finished writing a folk opera about the Poll Tax. We listened to old reel-to-reel tapes of some of his BBC radio documentaries. I was moved. This was a plus of city life that I could appreciate.

On the train going back to the hostel, Ellen was just able to prevent herself saying, "Well? What do you think of my London, now?" But it was written all over her face. I patted her hand. I didn't say it, but I would rather have been in the Plaza Bar.

We made new plans. I would go back to Cantilla in a couple of days. Jade had its first gig in a few days. She would come down in two weeks.. She would stay on for a while, and we could make up our minds then what to do next. The choices were just three: both of us in Cantilla, both of us in London, or both of us somewhere else, such as a new job in Africa. There was a fourth option which we didn't discuss. Neither of us could think about it.

Paco met me at Malaga Airport. It was a big expense, but worth it. I was carrying a suitcase made of folded canvas with framed pictures inside, plus a dozen items we couldn't find in Cantilla: a tea kettle, a reading backrest for the bed and a carved onyx Buddha for the mantle. Just necessities, really.

We drove through a world that seemed to be blessed with a different kind of light, as if the air itself was brighter. The turns of the mountain road were less terrifying, and the scenes from the summit made me gasp. Paco kept up a running commentary on Latigos, the sadly low price of almonds which the Americans had brought about through their market dumping, and stories of Moroccans streaming in to the greenhouses to take work from the honest Spanish labourers. None of it piqued my curiosity. My whole body seemed to be imbibing the Alpujarras like a dose of crucial medicine.

The mood lasted until we pulled into the Plaza where scaffolding had been erected in front of the *ayuntamiento*. Several workmen, including Guisado, were perched near the top of the wall, slapping cement into a recently excavated space.

"What's all that?" I asked Paco.

"Oh," he said. "I forgot. That's the new clock." He grinned broadly. "Better than the one in Latigos. It's electronic.," he finished, I thought reverently. I don't think he noticed me scowling.

Later, just as I was going to bed, the saccharine electronic notes of Big Ben rang out, followed by twelve bongs. It sounded like bad moog synthesiser stuff from the fifties. I looked at my watch, set to the infallible BBC. It was eleven fifty-one.

Chapter Twenty-three

Just A Little More Time

Spring doesn't come suddenly in the Alpujarras. One day you notice that you don't need to carry a sweater with you, and that the woodpile in the corral doesn't need any new logs. You realise that for weeks you have been walking through an explosion of wildflowers and hardly noticing. Every unploughed field and roadside verge is alive with poppies, buttercups, dandelions and little blue flowers whose names I never have found out. The grass heaves itself upward with such urgency and looks so succulent you think you could eat it yourself. All this green is framed against the almost unlikely blue of the mountain sky and the cap of snow on the slopes above.

It was Ellen who reminded me that spring had sprung. She was back for a visit, and she went around for the first two days saying "Ooooh" and "Ahhh" at every bend in the road. Having spent two months in London, she had lost her tan. She puffed a bit on the steep road up to Latigos when we went to buy bread. She accused me of having no aesthetic sensibility because I wasn't gasping with her at the sight of the valley's springtime excesses. I said anybody willing to live in a damp, grey city like London, where the sun went down at four o'clock, just for the sake of a career, was the pot calling the kettle *negro*. We were keeping it light.

It's not easy to get anything done in the Alpujarras. One morning you might get up early. You need, say, a pair of shoelaces from the general store in Latigos. While walking up the road, you see Aparicio, who says the owner of the old *bodega* in Latigos is getting rid of a load of wooden pallets from behind his shop. You follow him up the older, steeper farm track to the *paseo* and find Cecilio, who is stacking pallets onto his truck. You offer to buy them, but Cecilio says you can have them if you'll help him clean out the storeroom. Here you find six crudely blown glass bottles in rotting straw baskets that will be smashed and left in some *barranco*, so you add these to your haul. Now you have a truck full of stuff and no place to put it, so you ride with Cecilio down to Bill's, who is glad to share the booty and will store it all behind his house.

You realise it is now past noon. All the fresh bread will be gone if you don't hurry, so you puff back up the hill to one of the two bakeries. You use the socialist one at the bottom of Latigos, even through the bread is often better at the right-wing one in the plaza. You make this sacrifice for the sake of political solidarity. Charo, the owner of a shop, asks if you have seen Paco the postman this morning. He has already been to Latigos, but maybe not to Cantilla. She gives you a note to hand him if you see him, containing precise instructions for a pair of house slippers she wants him to bring her from Ugijar. She will pay him later. You start down the mountain again, but Manolo hails you from his *finca* along the road. He is the only farmer in this steep valley that keeps dairy cows. He wants to ask if you have heard anything about the government's new scheme to give away free solar energy panels for people who live outside the city limits. You have, because Bill has already applied for one. You help him write a letter on some paper torn from a cement sack. His daughter, Carmen, will print it out later on her portable typewriter. He gives you a two-litre Pepsi bottle full of milk.

Bill gets half the milk and you eat the bread that is growing cool under your arm with some goat's cheese he is trying to make. It is tangy and smells like wet sheep, but you are hungry. The dogs need de-ticking, so you hold them while Bill searches with needle-nosed pliers. They are ungrateful, and have to be bribed with cheese and the last of your bread. A horn blows from the road. It is Rafael, the dustman who collects garbage from along the road. A new rule from town hall says you have to raise the rubbish sacks above the ground so that dogs won't scatter it. He sits and smokes on his *dumper*, small tractor, and says that trout are being caught in the river below Bill's farm. We tie a sack of garbage in a pear tree. It is getting late. You need to find Gregorio, who had promised you a pile of *esparto* grass from his almond grove high up the slope. You hurry along the trail by the *acequia*, but get delayed by Jose, the lame shepherd, whose rams are head butting each other, streaming blood and testosterone, at the narrowest part of the path. While we wait, he tells you that trout have been caught in the river, even though it is still early in the year. You tell yourself to buy some fishhooks the next time you are in Latigos, which reminds you, just as you round the bend into your street: you have forgotten the shoelaces.

Bill and Aparicio were excited. The land at the bottom of Bill's farm was for sale. This was a large piece of at least five acres, but so steep and little-used that the name on the deed was "Finca Arrumbada," which means "neglected farm." There were three or four small terraces just below the *asequia* path, but most of the land was wild with brambles and an old poplar grove. The best thing was that the land had a thousand feet of frontage on the river, including our swimming hole. Aparicio said he could get the property for less than a hundred thousand pesetas, about seven hundred dollars.

I was getting used to the low prices of land around Cantilla, but this seemed incredible. The tract was a kind of nature reserve, overgrown so that birds used it for nesting and stopping places on their migratory pilgrimages. I had heard a pair of nightingales there once at night. By day, brilliant yellow bee-eaters soared and dived by the river. Sometimes you could catch sight of a hoopoe who had wandered off course from Morocco. The denseness of the forest and the steep incline made it look like the retreat of some Zen master even farther from home. Bill said he would put up the money, but that Ellen and I could share it. He had a plan: we would build a log cabin. There were hundreds of poplar trees, which were straight and tall. People referred to the land as the *alameda*, which means poplar grove. We could legally cut ten percent of the existing trees without needing a permit. Bill knew that I had helped build a log cabin some years before, in North Carolina. He was keen. It didn't matter if it took a long time, because what else had we got to do?

I looked at Ellen. She seemed to be trying to signal me, but about what I couldn't imagine. I agreed, shaking hands with Bill and Aparicio. They would go tomorrow to Bala Negra, on the coast, to make the purchase. Aparicio was sceptical about the cabin, since he had never seen one, but that didn't matter. The land had ten *celemines* of water attached to the deed. This was more water from the irrigation system than this wild plot would ever use. The water could be used anywhere downstream, by arrangement. The only problem, as far as Aparicio was concerned, was that, while Bill's farm was in the municipal limits of Latigos, the land we were buying belonged to Cantilla. Even better, I thought, but didn't say so.

On our way home, Ellen and I went along the *acequia*. The land was just as I remembered it. Mature poplars rose thirty metres from the river. They were budding now, and by June would cast shade over this whole bend of the river. Standing on the top terrace you could look over the edge of the stone wall to a sheer drop of more than a hundred feet. Even though we were only ten minutes brisk walk from Cantilla, there was no sound except the rush of wind in the poplars and the distant trickle of the river. The land on the other side of the stream was nearly vertical, a rock face broken by prickly pears clinging to ledges and cracks. The terraces could be cultivated, I said excitedly, the very place for the garden we had been planning all winter. There would be enough sunlight for that, at least.

Ellen was silent. There was so much we weren't talking about. We were back in the house, starting supper, before she spoke her mind. I had started to talk about the planned log cabin, but she interrupted me.

"Look, Art, I know you love this place. So do I. Maybe more. But it's time we decided what we're going to do."

"That again?" I asked, feeling my voice tighten. I peeled an onion and used my watering eyes as an excuse not to look at her.

"We bought this place. Fine. It's wonderful. It's…almost home for us now. But we can't… we can't make a whole life of it."

"Maybe this isn't the time to bring this up, Ellen," I said quickly, "but I've decided to write my book."

She sighed faintly. I had the impression that she was being careful with me.

"The novel, the one I talked about in the DR. Remember? The parable about the donkey and the…"

"Art, you haven't even taken the typewriter out of its case."

"So far I've just been thinking it through," I said, warming to the sound of my own words. "You've got to admit there's no better place in the world to write than Cantilla."

She got up and walked to the window, gazing at the stubble of new grass on Francisco's roof. "Are you really going to write it? I mean, really?"

My stomach hurt. I *had* been thinking about the book, but now I was being called on it.

"Yes," I said firmly, to both of us.

"Well, you can do that while I'm working with Peggy, then."

"Does that mean you're going to stay in London?" I asked as casually as possible.

"What else? I've got things I want to do, too."

"For a while," I said.

"Yes, for a while."

We ate in silence. Even I couldn't come up with chat. Before we turned in, Ellen said, "You can't stay here forever, you know."

"Who's talking about forever?" I replied. "I just want a little more time."

Chapter Twenty-four

Heroes and Star-Crossed Lovers

Once, riding back from a trip to Granada, Paco Taxista asked me, "Have you ever heard of Hero Braynad?"

"Who?"

"Hero Braynad. He's very famous."

"Never heard of him. What did he do?"

"He wrote books. He wrote one about Yegen."

"Oh! Gerald Brennan."

"That's what I said, Hero Braynad. Have you read his books?"

"One of them. The one you're talking about, *South from Granada.*"

"He was a *gilipolla*." This word, literally translated, means "a silly person," but in Andalucía it could be roughly equivalent to "asshole."

"Why? What did he do?"

Paco took his thick right hand off the steering wheel to tick off the points he was making. I wished he wouldn't do that on the mountain roads.

"One, he wrote things about some women from there that ruined their reputations. He made them sound like sluts."

"Were they?"

Paco scowled. "Whether they were or weren't that wasn't his business. That was their business. Their families' business. The pueblo's business." I kept quiet.

"Two, he insulted the community. He never really knew anybody very well except the people he hired to do his work. He hung around with nobody but *senoricos*."

This last word was the local term for *senoritos*, the minor *caciques*, or feudal landowners, that had used to own all the land in places like Cantilla. I had heard stories of the *senoricos* from some of the older men of the village. They remembered the days before the nineteen-fifties, when grown men could not own their own houses, when the landowner took half the crops, and when they had to "*tocar la gorra*," meaning "touch their caps" or salute the *senoricos* in the street. They were proud of the fact that they had expelled the landowners from the village forty years before, after Franco had abandoned the sharecropping system and its feudal privileges to concentrate on building an industrial base.

"Hero Braynad spent most of his time with the *senoricos*. How could he understand the village?"

"I see what you mean." Another thick finger was poised. "What's three?"

210

"Three," Paco said. He gave me a penetrating look, maybe a prescient one. "Arturo, do you know what the worst thing is?"

"Tell me."

"It's not him calling them ugly. If you're ugly, okay, you're ugly. If you're stupid, okay, you're stupid." He paused for effect. "The worst thing is not being ugly or stupid. The worst thing is being *funny*."

"I'll keep that in mind," I said.

Bill and Aparicio had gone to Bala Negra to buy the *alameda*. It was the last day before her flight, so Ellen and I took the car on a drive. We went through Latigos, down the twisty road past Jubar, with its absentee Japanese homeowners, past the steep village of Mairena and the valley where Mecinilla perches prettily over a river. Then through Valor, a prosperous-looking place with a new plantation of palms lining the high street. We were high on the breast of the Sierra, looking across the Alpujarra valley to the clusters of white villages on the opposite slope of the Contraviesa. The air was perfectly clear, and we strained our eyes for a glimpse of Morocco, but saw only the mirrored sunlight of the Mediterranean. Our mood was light, as if we were on vacation, and we didn't talk about next year at all.

The village of Yegen, made famous by Brennan, is an unprepossessing place, spilling down the hill from the highway. We parked at a bar built on the road whose purpose was clearly to attract passing truck drivers and, if there should happen to be any, tourists making a pilgrimage to Brennan's house. It was closed. There was no sign indicating the direction of the house, so we walked down a steep street, past a fountain in a small square. I asked a woman for directions. She was pushing a wheelbarrow laden with newly harvested broad beans. She didn't seem surprised when I asked her where Brennan's house was, just inclined her head in the direction from which we had just come. I turned to see a bronze plaque bolted to the wall of a house in need of paint. It said that this was the home of the writer Gerald Brennan, and gave the years of residence in the nineteen-twenties.

The house was plainly unoccupied. It was substantial building that would have belonged to a family of importance, because it was large and because of its situation near the fountain. There was no sign of recent occupation. An aged yellow dog lay in a strip of shade by the door. We stood back and craned our necks for a while, but I couldn't really put it together with the passages from the book. In this house, the mad and talented Dora Carrington had sketched the hills of the valley. The brilliant and disconsolate Virginia Woolf had sat looking out from the *azotea*, or attic, above us. And the delicate Lytton Strachey, complaining of flea bite and rough food, had somehow been induced to ride for days in an open wagon to be in Yegen. The cream of the Bloomsbury group, here due to the persuasive obsession of Gerald Brennan.

The few people who passed on their errands ignored us. We wouldn't be so rare, I realised. But as we added nothing to the economy or the pleasure of village life, we were irrelevant. There was nothing to indicate that I was a *buena persona*, a fellow resident of these mountains, a speaker, more or less of the language. The impression I got was that Hero Braynad was not hated, as Paco had claimed, nor revered, as remote readers of his famous book would imagine, but just another fact in the multitude of facts that had constituted life in this place for a thousand years. The unfairly treated female servant, the egregious *senorico*, the lustre of the famous visitors and now Gerald Brennan himself, interred at last in Malaga, were of no more consequence than the dog who lay scratching in the road. The endless fact of the pueblo outweighed all this, as it would outweigh our own present concerns about the future. The dog yawned. We left.

If you stay on the high mountain road you will arrive at Trevelez, a village that at one time enjoyed the reputation of being the highest in Europe. This changed, we were told, when some damned French built a skiing town somewhere in the Alps. Trevelez lies at the end of what has to be the most extreme detour possible. You drive up a road that is really an enormous hairpin bend. For miles you can see the road winding back the way you are driving, along the sides of a steep ravine. When you arrive, you find a good-sized village straddling the ravine across a fast flowing river. The air is cool, even in summer, because of the altitude. This is where people want their cured hams to come from. Because there is snow about much of the winter, the flies die early. Hams can hang in storage barns not much above the temperature of refrigerators. It is where people send their own recently slaughtered meat to cure. It is true; the best *jamon serrano* comes from there.

If you stay with the highway, you will come to the large village of Orgiva, together with Lanjaron, probably the best-known places in the Alpujarras. Orgiva has been well settled with foreigners over the years. If you want to see a few survivors of the hippie era, that is the place to look. A counter culture has been born there of artists, spiritual seekers and nature lovers. The views are magnificent, stretching across the river valley to the shadowed shoulders of the coastal range. You can sit in a pavement café drinking *cappuccino* if you wish, or enrol in a course of self-improvement in a residential centre. You can do yoga, primal screaming or painting of Jungian archetypes. You can buy a *finca* from estate agents who understand what foreigners need, and have prices to match. It is a very pleasant place to spend an afternoon.

In the hills nearby there is a village which enjoys what must be a unique honour. One day in the nineteen-eighties a small group of robed Tibetan monks arrived from their place of exile in northern India. They were following occult signs which led them to believe that a small boy of this village was the reincarnation of an important lama who had died a few years before. Various children were interviewed, to the bemusement of locals, until one child—let us call him Pepe—correctly identified some objects that had belonged to the deceased lama. After negotiations with the parents and the authorities baby Pepe and his mother were taken to India, where he was brought up and educated in the ways of Tibetan Buddhism.

The national press got hold of the story while I was spending my first winter in Cantilla. Pictures of the child and his mother appeared in *Hola!* Magazine, bringing temporary and not much wanted fame to the village. Now grown up, Pepe has been enthroned as a lama of high standing. He and his mother divide their time between India and Granada. There have been some problems. The family wasn't able to maintain its integrity in these odd circumstances. The final outcome will be interesting to watch, but none of this has done anything to tarnish the reputation of the western, and more developed, Alpujarras as a place of spiritual importance. Places like Cantilla, too remote for most enthusiasts, still wallow in their protective obscurity.

We crossed the valley and headed for the coast, craning our necks like any tourist at the scenery. Passing through a tunnel, we descended to Albunol, a hot agricultural town at the top of an immense *rambla*, or river bed, that runs all the way to the sea. We made for Castell de Ferro, a former fishing village recently colonised by foreigners wanting cheap seaside real estate. It is a pretty place with coves of shingled beaches. Small fishing boats, bucking the trend of the dying fishing industry, still went out daily to catch *pescaitos*, the small fry much loved by Andalucians. There were still posts anchored on the beach with winches to drag the boats onshore. Even in this early spring weather a few people were swimming and sunning themselves. We parked and took our shoes off and waded in the shallows as the sun began to dip in the sky.

We ate in a small restaurant built right on the beach. Ellen, not a fan of seafood, stayed with chicken, but I ate a *paella* that can only be described as a symbolic representation of the depths, an almost Freudian experience of creatures so recently swimming that I felt the need to dispatch the tendrils with my fork. It was delicious. I stretched out on the bonnet of the car and dozed while Ellen sketched the scene in pastels. They went well, because she showed me a couple of pictures. When the shadows lengthened on the beach, we drove home. Neither of us said it, but the end of the day seemed like the end of something else as well.

Ellen packed early for her five a.m. departure. She would ride with Paco to the bus station in Granada, then take an express coach to the Malaga airport. She was travelling light, so she had bought a few things to take with her as gifts. I was in the kitchen when she called out, "Art, bring me that *chorizo*, will you?"

"Where is it?"

"On the table by the window in a yellow plastic bag."

There was nothing on the table except a short stack of paperback books and an umbrella. The window was ajar.

"What do you want first, the bad news or the bad news?" I called.

She was standing in the doorway. "The Cat?" she asked.

"The Cat," I said.

The book wasn't coming. The story, which had made such sense in my head, couldn't make it down my arms and fingers to the keypad. I had written before, even sold a few short stories. I had never had writer's block, because I only wrote when I felt like it. Now that Ellen was in London my relationship with the typewriter seemed to be my last best link with Cantilla.

When I spoke long distance to Ellen, turning to the wall in Rosario's shop, I tried not to sound defensive. She wasn't interrogating me about my progress, but I felt that I had to sound engaged with the work. She did with hers; she was making a small career for herself in the folk music world of London. She had been chosen as one of the singers in residence at Cecil Sharpe House, that refuge of sandal-wearers and idealists. I tried to sound positive, but when I hung up, a sense of bleakness threatened to overwhelm me.

Bill didn't pry, but I noticed he was not mentioning Ellen. We spent a lot of time with Aparicio, who wasn't so sensitive. He joked that I was now a bachelor, and should take advantage of it. He rattled off a list of women's names that were longing for companionship. Most of these were fictional, I'm sure. I joked back, but it wasn't funny.

That must have been how Lola's name came up. The three of us were standing on the newly purchased land, calculating how far down the river was by using an old Boy Scout trick I had remembered using your thumb and a notched stick. Aparicio told the story.

Road works had been underway just below Ugijar a year or so ago. The company with the contract had brought in its own workers, as was the custom. About a dozen men from Murcia had been staying in the hostel in Ugijar. Somehow, one of these had met Lola, the pretty and confused woman from Cantilla that I had seen during the fiesta, and had pursued her for days, borrowing a truck from his boss and parking outside Cantilla for several nights. No one knew exactly how things had happened, but he had become infatuated with Lola, left his job and rented a house in Mairena. One night Jose had come home from a friend's house to find a note on his kitchen table, saying that Lola had found her true life partner, whose name was Enrique, and had decided to leave home. She was sorry that things had not worked out. The children were with the neighbours. She would send money to help with support when Enrique found a new job. She loved them very much, but her heart was clear: Enrique was her soul mate.

Jose went back to his mother's house. He wept. She was white-lipped with fury, but still managed a look of satisfaction: she had always known this would happen. She had chided Jose over the years each time Lola came home late, wearing a flushed complexion and mumbling excuses. The softness of her eyes did not fool anyone. She sent for Rodrigo, her eldest son, leaving Jose on the couch.

There were hushed consultations. Rodrigo went to the plaza bar and spoke quietly to his brother-in-law. Word spread. Men didn't go home. Drink flowed. Everyone waited for Rodrigo to make the suggestion. This he did, not long past nine o'clock. Men left the bar in groups and went through the streets of the village, knocking on doors, returning with kitchen pans, metal buckets and hammers. Plastic bottles were filled with wine. All the cars in the village filled quickly as the men left Cantilla. The women said nothing, but their faces were alight with dread and moral satisfaction; the men had gone to Mairena.

Aparicio paused and lit a cigarette. He was teasing us, we could see. It was Bill who said, finally, "And?"

"And they did what any pack of fools will do, tanked up on wine. They found the house where this Enrique was staying. They yelled and shouted and threatened. They drank wine and swore and started beating the pots and pans so that no one in Mairena could get any sleep. They stayed there all night."

"What happened?" I asked him. "What about the guy?"

217

Aparicio couldn't keep a sardonic grin off his face. "Still in Murcia, I'd say."

"And Lola?"

"Lola? She's back home. She always goes back home."

Chapter Twenty-five

Water Fights

The world was drying up. The sky turned white as the sun rose to the mid-heavens. The siesta that had taken place between two and five had lengthened; nobody was about between one and six o'clock, when the men led their damp-looking animals slowly to the fields. Finally having mastered the art of keeping the house cool, I stayed inside reading and swatting flies all afternoon, or spent the day sitting in the river below the *alameda*.

It had not rained since April. Once or twice the sky clouded over, but the sun burned through by afternoon, leaving behind a humid funk that was even more uncomfortable. I had expected it to be dry, but it began to seem somehow more threatening, like the two-year drought I had seen in Botswana, when people began to go hungry and cows died in the outskirts of the village from lack of grass.

The river was still flowing, but its volume had shrunk so that no one had trouble fording it at the sides of the temporary bridges. The water level for the *acequias* had begun to falter. From dawn until after dark people could be seen hoeing open channels on their terraces to allow the thin streams of water onto their crops. It soaked away immediately, leaving crusts on the small ridges that divided the rows. The *asequero*, a man named Ricardo, who had been elected to allocate the water and oversee its distribution, began to avoid the bar. Too many people had complaints and special requests. Cantilla was too small a place to stay truly impartial.

No one spoke of anything else. A woman told me that even the almond trees, very resistant to drought, had begun to fail. The *nacimientos*, or springs, had begun to dry up. There had been too small a cap of snow on the Sierras this winter, and the places where water had flowed all day as if from an open tap were now just showing trickles. There were rumours that the provincial government was going to declare rationing for household use in Latigos. This was ominous, because it meant that the farmers uphill were getting desperate. Soon they might try their old trick of diverting Cantilla's water under cover of darkness. Cantilleros avoided the market and stood apart in the queue at the doctor's surgery. They caught hard looks from the *Gallegos.* There was a feeling of impending trouble; you could see it in everyone's eyes.

Aparicio showed it too. He was quiet and withdrawn as the three of us met one morning at seven to water Bill's fields. We were already beginning to perspire when the Latigos *asequero*, a taciturn young man with a clipboard, arrived to open the *acequia* exactly on time. In these days of drought, minutes were important. No one could make jokes about "Spanish time." We moved the sheet metal gate at the top of Bill's land and let the water flow into an earth channel we had cleared the day before. There was no point in watering weeds on the way down. I thought the *asequero* gave me a hard look. I was, in some sense, a Cantillero, and he knew it. Bill told me I was getting paranoid.

Bill's farm had an allotment of fifteen *celemines,* the basic unit of irrigation. This meant that he could take from the shared irrigation channel all the water that would flow during a set period of time. Each *celemin* was counted in minutes. In April, a *celemin* had been twelve minutes, so that Bill could count on about three hours whenever it was his turn. He could pour the water on his land, or store it in the large cement tank we sometimes used as a swimming pool. Now a *celemin* was worth only four minutes, a figure arrived at during a meeting of farmers in Latigos a week earlier. What was worse, Bill's turn came up every nine days instead of every week, as before. He had heard that the farmers had spoken of Cantilla in bitter voices, because their *celemines* were eight minutes, and their turns once a week.

We led the water into Bill's garden, where it sank immediately between the rows of vegetables and flowers. We filled the lily pond, and the dogs clambered in, drinking and splashing noisily. There was enough for the ornamental shrubs, but we quickly saw that there would be little or none left for the olive terraces below. Aparicio said that the trees would be all right, but that the olive crop was cut in half each time the trees missed watering. If Bill had been reliant on the trees and their oil for survival, as farmers had been in years past, there would be real reason to worry.

Naively, I asked if we couldn't pump the water from the poplar grove we had just bought up to the lower terraces of Bill's farm. Aparicio rolled his eyes. Bill explained that, in the Alpujarras, water could never be lifted, except for household use. The *acequias* functioned by gravity and gravity was their law. Any drop that fell could be used on its way down, but what extra there might be belonged to people downhill. It was a rule so basic that everyone, even children, accepted it as naturally as they did the basic laws of human behaviour: you don't steal people's things, and you don't pump water.

We were finished by the time the sun cleared the mountain to the east. The *asequero* appeared as promptly as before, and we watched him close the water gate. Another farmer would be standing in his rubber boots somewhere downhill, waiting his turn. We watched the water flow by. I had a sense of the absurdity of something so simple becoming something so precious. The water that ran unheeded from my hose while washing my car in years past, the water flowing unchecked while I shaved, the sprinklers drenching the earth of suburban split levels of my childhood. There was real reason to fear drought here. The meteorologists said so, the radio newscasts droned on about it. No one in the Alpujarras needed to be told.

We spent the rest of the morning at the *alameda*. Bill had brought some bread and *chorizo* and we lunched by the river. Bill and I sat in the water, but Aparicio rode away. He had been behaving strangely all day. I asked Bill if he was ever seen wet. He shook his head and joked that, like the Wicked Witch of the East, he might dissolve in water. In the shade of the trees by the river we were unaware that the thermometer was touching a hundred degrees for the fifth day in a row. We also missed the crowd of men outside the plaza bar, already drinking on a day when they had stayed home from work, talking in increasingly dire voices about the men of Latigos, and what they had done to the main water canal at four o'clock that morning.

Deeds for water use are under constant dispute in the Alpujarras. From the smallest complaint of a farmer about his neighbour's allocation of *celemines* to major court battles concerning the diversion of springs high in the Sierra to the greenhouses of El Ejido, the subject is an unending source of tension.

Cantilla had two major sources of water. The most important was described in a deed that went back four hundred years. This said that all the water that flowed in the river during the hours of darkness belonged to the village, and that water that flowed during daylight went downstream to Cherin. Even though the river flowed through the land in the municipality of Latigos, none of it could be used on their land. The second source was a major spring high up the mountain below Bayarcal, which was divided between Latigos and Cantilla by a complex formula that led to much confusion. There was a stone building with a large diverting valve built inside. The operation of this was shared by the *asequeros* of the two villages. Each had a key to unlock the building, and each had a copy of the rules. Surprisingly, their roles seemed usually to overcome their loyalties to their pueblos. It was not unlike the red telephones that linked the Kremlin and the White House; the sheer enormity of the task ennobled the functionaries.

Paco Junior told me what had happened. He kept his voice low as he spoke and leaned forward conspiratorially. During the night someone had broken the lock on the building that housed the valve and had diverted Cantilla's water into the storage tank above Latigos. When the *asequero* from Cantilla had arrived at six, he had found his opposite number sitting glumly in the doorway. Words had been exchanged. Ricardo had accused the Latigos *asequero* of being involved. When the Latigos *asequero* left, Ricardo had nailed the door shut, with the valve open to Cantilla's storage tank. He had returned an hour later to find the door ripped open and hanging off its hinges, the water diverted once again. He sent for a few friends, and they were now guarding the building with axe handles and bricks, determined to remain in place until the sun set, when they would reclaim their missing two hours of water. A crowd had gathered in the plaza of Latigos. Charo, the wife of a shop owner who had been born in Cantilla, but who, unusually, had married a man from Latigos, telephoned Remedio's store. Cantilleros were now gathering in a warlike mood.

I had felt uncomfortable anyway. The men I knew were cool in their greetings as I entered the bar. They were unshaven and drunk. No one stood next to me. I realised that they were preparing to drive en masse to the switch house when sunset neared. They would defend the water for at least their two hours, but I felt that it wouldn't end there. These men looked as if they had dispensed with rules. They might be there all night.

Francisco was on his stoop when I got home. He had his usual bottle of wine open beside him, but he wasn't smiling. He told me the story of what had happened again, but I heard that, as in a game of Chinese Whispers, the hours had stretched and the culpability of the Latigos farmers had grown. The mysterious force of shared opinion was working its way through Cantilla. Even the women were sombre. It was possible to feel something like fear afoot.

I was worried about what might be expected of me when things got started. I wondered what would have happened if Lola had pulled her great escape while we were living in

Cantilla. Would the men have come by for me? It was one more of those small paradoxes that highlighted our foreignness in the village. I sat nervously at the kitchen table, waiting. It was going to be a long night.

Sundown came. No one had knocked on my door. I went into the street and looked around. There were no men in sight and the women had closed their shutters. Even the dogs, prescient in every emergency, were nowhere to be seen. I went to the plaza, but found the door of the bar locked. Gregorio was sitting quietly with another pensioner in a doorway. I greeted him, and was relieved to see him smile. Only the old and the foreign were left, it seemed.

About ten o'clock I could hear noise in the street. Jose and Francisco wobbled arm and arm to the front of the house. I leaned out.

"Hey, Arturo!" shouted Francisco. "Come on over, have a drink."

"Thanks anyway," I said. "What happened?"

"They chickened out! The *Gallegos* chickened out," said Jose. Craning his neck to look up at my window made him stagger.

"It's over, then?"

Francisco snorted. "It never started. They know better, don't they, Jose? They know better than to mess around with Cantilleros."

Aparicio was full of good cheer the next morning. We were weeding the new flower beds under the pergola and all except he were eating green figs from the first crop of the year. He told us that the mayors of the two villages had called a meeting at the switch house. The Cantilleros just stood around swigging wine, having left their axe handles in the cars. The two *asequeros* would have new locks installed. Everyone was to shake hands all around. Two bored *civiles* leaned against their car and watched while this was done. Another summer, another anti-climax, it seemed.

"They knew they were in the wrong," said Aparicio scornfully. "Cantilleros are all talk."

I was surprised to find that I was annoyed. It was less easy to go along with Aparicio's scorn for my neighbours these days. Maybe group opinion had grabbed me, too. I didn't say anything, but thought, "Typical Gallego bullshit," and felt better.

Chapter Twenty-six

Why the Swallows Come Back to Capistrano

Bill and I paced off the dimensions of the log cabin. It would fit snugly against a stone wall on the lowest of the terraces, perched a hundred feet above the river. There was enough room for a small patio and some steps leading to the larger terraces above. It would have a view up the river, facing Bayarcal and the Sierra peaks. It would be twelve feet square. We drove stakes at the four corners under the sceptical eye of Aparicio. He wanted to know how many trees we would have to cut. I worked it out with a ballpoint on a paper bag.

"Okay, we need four logs measuring about fourteen feet per course. Each course will measure, what, about eight inches? The walls will be eight feet high, and the floor joists will take up another two courses. Leaving out spaces for the door and the window, that's, let's see, four times fourteen. If we get two logs out of each tree, that's..."

"Twenty-eight trees," said Bill. I multiplied again. He was right.

"That's a lot of trees," said Aparicio.

"There must be, what, thirty or forty up there." I pointed up the slope. "We couldn't cut them all, of course."

"There are a lot more down the slope," said Bill hopefully.

"Who's going to carry them up?" asked Aparicio. "And what about the branches and the waste bits? You can't just leave them lying on the ground."

I shot him a deadly ray from my eye. All this logic was threatening to ruin my morning.

"Bricks," said the cynic Aparicio, chucking a stone in the direction of the river. "That's what you want. The bugs will eat the poplar logs in one year."

"Not if you treat them," I said, feeling the project slip away even further.

"There's a guy in Mecina Bombaron that sells poplar logs, isn't there, Aparicio?" Bill asked.

Aparicio grunted. Bill and I wanted a log cabin, and that's what we would have.

We dug a stairway out of the bank. It was so steep that we had to put in two switchbacks to make it work out. We dragged down flat stones from the steep wall by the *acequia* and set them in place and fit them into the cut earth. Aparicio cleared the brambles from the terrace with his sickle. By noon we had the basics of a construction site. I was sweaty and happy.

"Helloooo!" came a voice from above us. I turned to see the freshly washed faces of Richard and Susan leaning over the *acequia*.

"I say," said Richard, "It is steep down here, isn't it?"

"I forgot to tell you," said Bill innocently. "They've come back to buy a house in Cantilla."

Paco Taxista, as it turned out, had a house for sale. It was a good big place overlooking the veranda and the bottom of the village not far from our road. We met him in the Plaza bar when he got back from Granada. He rummaged around in his house until he found a key, like ours, a big clunky antique that you could also use as a bottle opener. The four of us pushed the door open in the twilight. Dodging cobwebs, Paco found the fuse for the electricity. I saw that the entryway and corral were larger than ours, and felt a stab of envy.

Upstairs, a large room opened with double French windows onto a balcony looking across steps of descending terraces to the river. The kitchen had an old refrigerator that hummed promisingly. There were two large bedrooms. The *camara* had been divided, and there was an extra room at the back.

"Look, Richard," Susan purred. "Your darkroom."

I had had talks with Ellen about my negative attitude to other foreigners. I had had to admit that it was irrational. Ellen had said that I was trying to make Cantilla into the perfect hideaway, an unspoilt Big Rock Candy Mountain. It wasn't and would never be. Trying to create it in my own image would only lead to grief. Even though I was forced to agree with her, I couldn't help feeling bleak as the perfectly nice couple made their plans for Paco's house.

We went back to the bar. Paco's accent was a little too thick for Susan, so I was doing translations. Richard sidled up next to me.

"Let's talk man to man, Art," he said.

"Shoot," I muttered and took a big gulp of wine.

"Can we trust this fellow?" he asked. His face was conspiratorial. We were two white men discussing an African village. We know the natives can be tricky; you could really only trust your own kind. I wanted to teach him a lesson. I wanted to say, "The question, my dear Mr. Stanley, is whether he can trust you." Looking at his face, I saw that he was innocent. He was only doing what he knew best. A time would come when he would wince at the memory of asking me such a thing. At least, I hoped so.

"Yes, you can," was all I said.

The deal was struck before we left the bar. Susan was flushed with excitement. She kissed me on the cheek. They would be so happy here, she knew. It was all thanks to me that they had found this place. She and Richard and Ellen and I were going to be great friends. They would be visiting here every chance they got, working on the house, getting ready for Richard's retirement. They would be back tomorrow. Right now they were going back to their hotel to call their family in Bristol.

"Tell the barman I want to pick up the tab for these drinks," he told Susan as they turned to go.

I shook my head. "Paco has already paid," I said. That was something else he would have to learn.

I went home. Guisado would be at me first thing in the morning, I knew. I could feel the pings of his profit radar already.

Bill and I had been peeling logs for weeks. Poplar needs to cure for at least a year before being used. If it is not, the predatory flying wood beetles, *polillas*, will eat it. The little terrace in the Alameda was stacked high with peeled logs. We would work for a while and then swim in the river. Bill kept a bottle of shampoo there on a flat rock, and I left a razor as well.

In the heat of Cantilla a hot shower was the last thing you wanted. Recognising real priorities, we had built a stone barbecue on the future cabin patio, and often didn't go home to eat. We would bring ribs and chops from Remedio's shop when she had them, sardines from the travelling fish vendor when she didn't. Bill was awash with fresh vegetables and his own olive oil. We wrapped potatoes in foil and ate like royalty, letting the long day end as we lay in the grass.

But one day something was the matter with Hippie. Bill turned up with just Sadi at his side. He said Hippie had been off his food the day before, and this morning he had refused to get up from his corner of the porch. He had been whimpering and trying to nibble at his hindquarters. He had always seemed a very robust sort of dog, one that would follow you into town and see off even the biggest competitors for *tapa* scraps in the bar. He often went missing for a day or two, returning famished and thirsty, and, inevitably, a new crop of curly-haired pups followed a few months later. It seemed unlikely that anything could be seriously wrong, so I made a joke about too much procreation. Bill didn't laugh.

We worked in silence. Bill was wrapped up in his mood, and I was brooding about the new English invasion of Cantilla. I told Bill what Richard had had the gall to say about Paco Taxista.

"It was unbelievable. He actually thought Paco might cheat him."

"So?" He'll learn about these things, just like you did."

"Oh yeah? I'll believe that when I see it." I scraped at my log with extra force. "I'm telling you, Bill, they're part of the first wave of English sightseers. In a few years this valley will be full of them. You'll see fish and chip shops and souvenir stalls from here to Almeria"

"So...? What are you going to do about that? If a place like this is as wonderful as you think it is, why shouldn't other people come?"

This kind of talk wasn't like Bill. At least, I didn't think so. For a moment I wondered if I had just assumed that Bill shared my reluctance to open up Cantilla to the hordes. I kept quiet, and some of the brightness went out of the morning.

It didn't take Bill very long to pursue his point. Maybe it was his concern for Hippie, or maybe I was really starting to get on his nerves.

"What you're trying to do is keep this place just like you found it. You're trying to cast it in...what do you call it? Aspic."

"Amber," I said dryly.

"Whatever. Anyway, it seems to me that you don't like the way things are going around here," he said, without stopping his work. "Every day you've got some new complaint." I reddened.

"You don't like people coming here to live. You don't like the greenhouses people want to build to make a living. You don't even like the new clock. Have I left anything out?"

"Just one thing," I said, getting to my feet. "I don't like being turned on by my friends."

"Art..."

"Forget it," I said, and after an embarrassing, unathletic scramble up the bank, walked home.

.

As the weather got even hotter I learned why the swallows, in the words of the song, always came back to Capistrano. The reason was flies. In a village like Cantilla, where every house had a pig in the basement and a horse or mule for transport, flies were inevitable. The *golondrinas,* swallows, are the first line of defence. They nest in the cracks in your walls and invade your attics, leaving steaks of droppings everywhere, but in the afternoon they wheel and soar like guided missiles through the hot air, consuming flies by the million.

In summer you learn that your house is not so much an object as a machine. Every detail of the traditional construction has been tried and proven over centuries, and woe to the foreigner who thinks it would be nice to put in large bedroom windows, say, or a skylight. The sun is the enemy. The chief motive for the hordes of tourists' annual pilgrimages to the Costa Del Sol is the single greatest problem for the residents. As they say in Andalucía, the best thing about the sun is shade. Your house is painted white, not because it's charming, but because it reflects sunlight. Does your bedroom lack a window? That's how it should be; where there is darkness there is cool air. Do you fling open your shutters to greet the morning sun? Not if you want to be able to sleep that night. You leave shutters closed, drape *persianas* across any opening and let the mass of the stone walls cling to the cool of the night air. Do you put insulation in your roof? Not unless you want to spend the summer beneath a giant tea cosy. The best thing to do is let the heat out of the attic at sundown.

It didn't take me long to learn all this. A few weeks sitting in the kitchen with a can of bug spray and a flyswatter taught me rapidly. I hung a heavy beaded fly curtain over the front door in June. It made a lovely musical sound when you passed through it, and it made our house look just like the neighbours'. The back bedroom was kept cool by leaving the windows shut all day, the opposite of what you might expect. From June to late September you do not so much occupy your house as pilot it.

I was missing Ellen. There was no getting around it. Bill's apparent defection had made an even larger hole in my world, and I was having a hard time filling it. I called her daily, grimly paying Remedio's outrageous telephone charges. She seemed remote, as if I were already part of her past life. I saved up stories about people in Cantilla, but I usually didn't have the heart to tell them. Each time I rang off, I put an artificial smile on my face and went straight home.

One sweltering evening, Ismael, Remedio's youngest son knocked on my door. There was a call for me in the shop, a full two hours before the charges got lower. I ran after him, sweating litres and gasping unashamedly. It was Ellen.

"I just called," she said, "to say…"

"I know," I said. "I love you, too."

"No, I mean I *do* love you, Art. You know that. But I called to say that Ewan has collapsed. He's in hospital. Peggy is very worried. He's got, you know, a heart thing."

"Attack."

"Yes. A heart attack. I think he's bad."

I couldn't respond. Despite being a man of seventy-odd years, Ewan McColl seemed indestructible. I realised that it meant different things to the two of us. To me it was concern over the health of a friend, but to Ellen it must have seemed to be the threat of the end of the world. She had been revolving around Peggy and Ewan during the weeks she had been in London, and it must have seemed as if the earth had shifted. I took a deep breath.

"Do you want me to come?" I asked.

There was a moment's silence. "I guess not. I just wanted to…you know, tell you. There's nothing you can do here."

"Except support you."

"I feel better already. It's that things like this, well, you want to be with your family."

I realised that my eyes were stinging. Not about Ewan, though that was sad enough, but because, for the first time in months, Ellen was really talking to me.

"Give them my love. Tell Peggy I'll call tomorrow," I said.

I went up the other side of the valley at sundown. I knew just where I wanted to be. There was a crumbling old *cortijo* at the highest point of the hill, above the *secano*, where the water didn't reach. A couple of huge palm trees were hanging on for dear life in the dry soil. They would have been planted when some long-ago couple were married, to mark the occasion. No one in the village would remember the people or the wedding, but life would have been lived here, children born and crops harvested, dances danced and tears shed. The palms, all that remained of the life, were tokens of this. I sat on a broken stone wall and looked across the valley at Cantilla.

I had memorised the streets of the village, and, as I looked, I had a memory of each corner. There was our house, with its slightly yellower high stone rear wall, belly bulging over the church's vacant lot. There was the balcony at Remedio's shop. The youngest daughter, Lupe, was taking down washing. There was the wide place in the street where the pig had met his end, and the building from which Manolito had dived. Paco Taxista's taxi was parked on the road above the church. Some early teenage couples were walking up the hill by the school for some clandestine necking. A man too far away to recognise was walking behind his laden mule up the path from the river, hanging with both hands from the animal's tail.

Ellen and I had come here together; I to find something I still couldn't put a name to, and she simply to be with me. Now we were a thousand miles apart, and, search as I did in the dying light of the day, I couldn't find any reason why.

Chapter Twenty-seven

Lost and Found

Aparicio would rather be caught dead than be seen in Cantilla. So I was more than surprised when I heard a horse stop in front of my house the next afternoon and looked down out of the window at his cloth-capped head. I invited him in. He didn't dismount. Maybe he thought that was too much of a commitment.

"No, Arturo, I just came to tell you that Bill needs some help. His dog—the big yellow one—it looks like he's dying. Bill wants to take him to a doctor over in Cadiar."

"Hasn't he got a car?" I said, surprising myself with the coldness in my voice.

Aparicio grinned with embarrassment. "He wants you to drive him, so that he can hold the dog," he said. "But, of course, if you can't…"

"Don't be ridiculous," I said.

Bill was standing with Hippie in his arms at the top of his drive. The dog's curly hair was matted with sweat, and Bill had wrapped him in a towel. He got in and I handed him the bundle, thinking that he felt smaller than before. Sadi was whimpering and growling beside the car. We took off in silence along the rutted road to Ugijar. Whenever we hit a bump, Hippie yelped. Bill's face was set and stoical. I couldn't think what to say.

We got to Cadiar at just about nightfall. There were no veterinarians for dogs in the Alpujarras, just a visiting government one for livestock, whose office was in Motril. The doctor of a human clinic, a friend of a friend, had agreed to see what could be done for Hippie after surgery hours. We parked and sat on a bench near the town fountain with the dog at our feet.

"Aparicio says he must have swallowed a chicken bone," said Bill woodenly. "He was always a whore for the tapas."

We laughed insincerely. The swelling at Hippie's backside was all too obvious. He hadn't eaten and hardly moved since the day Bill and I had had our disagreement by the cabin. He was clearly not long for this world.

The doctor admitted us through a rear door. He explained that if people were to see him treating a dog that he would be denounced to the local government. Despite his weakness,

237

Hippie tried to bite him as we set him carefully on the operating table. The doctor took a cursory look, then grunted.

"It's probably in his intestines," he said. "The only thing we can do is open him up."

He prepared an injection. None of us knew how much morphine to give him, so the medic measured out a child's dose. Hippie rested his head on Bill's palm and only yelped slightly as the injection went in. By the time the doctor readied his instruments to shave Hippie's hair, he had stopped breathing. Bill put his hands uselessly on the dog's chest as if to start resuscitation, but the doctor shook his head. We carried the bundle back to the car without a word, and started home in the dark.

"He was just a dog," Bill said. "I've been through lots worse than this."

"That's right," I answered.

"I mean, I was there when my mother died. I was only twelve."

"That was lots worse, sure."

"Then why…" Bill started, but I saw that he couldn't finish his sentence.

We got Hippie home about eleven o'clock. The evening was bright with stars, and we had no trouble digging a grave in the centre of a stone platform Bill intended to encircle a walnut tree. Sadi sniffed around curiously for a while, then went to sleep at Bill's feet. I went inside and got a Pepsi bottle of wine and we passed it back and forth. Bill was no drinker, but he managed at least half a bottle.

"To Hippie!" he shouted after a while. "To the best goddamn horniest, toughest, most disobedient sneaky, loveable wretch in the valley!"

"To Hippie!" I agreed, and without any self-consciousness, we gave each other a hug.

Ewan was recovering from his heart attack. I could hear the relief in Ellen's voice when I called her the next afternoon. Peggy and some friends had gathered around his hospital bed, annoying the nurses until he was put into a private room. This was signal for the whole group to start singing.

Ellen said that when Ewan and Peggy reached the casualty ward, one of the first things the doctors asked him was if he smoked.

"No," said Ewan.

"You liar," said Peggy.

Ewan smiled. "I just quit," he said.

Ellen and Peggy were practising again. Jade now had four voices. They had played a few gigs, but bookings were hard to come by. I thought I heard a note of uncertainty in her voice.

"How are you *really*?" I dared to ask.

She hesitated. "I don't know, Art. Maybe it's this damn rain. It hasn't stopped since I got back."

"Nice and hot here," I said carefully.

"Yeah, well, it's not just the weather. I miss you, too."

"Cantilla's not the same, either."

"I'm not talking about Cantilla. I'm talking about us."

"I miss us, too."

There was an expensive silence as I waited on Remedio's piratical telephone. I tried to look engaged. There was a small queue of village women behind me waiting their turn.

"Art, can I check into some jobs for us?"

"What kind of jobs?"

"Well, there's something coming up in Bolivia. I met the director of a village development project here. He says our qualifications are just what he wants. The funding is in place and all."

I fought back an urge to groan.

"But there's something else, too. The Mennonites have got a really interesting position in north Kenya, working with some Maasai."

The women behind me were fixing me with an unkind glare. I squirmed. I thought of five or six good reasons to say no.

"Sure, Ellen," I said. "Go ahead."

As I walked home I thought about what she had said. I could tell that, without her close relationship with Peggy, her enthusiasm for London, perhaps for living on her own, was beginning to wane. But I could also tell that she didn't just want to come back to Cantilla, even to be with me. She was invoking our old code, the one that had sustained us through all the years and foreign countries. She wanted us to go back to work. And for the first time in months, I thought she might be right.

When I came down Calle del Rio, I found Francisco sitting on his stoop, holding his much bigger child in his lap. There was a bottle of wine beside him. I saw to my surprise that he had been weeping.

"What's the matter?" I asked.

"You know that cat, Arturo, the one that made me fall?"

"Yes. Why? Have you seen him?"

"I killed him," choked Francisco, and burst into a fresh flood of tears. I sat down on the stoop, not knowing whether to pat him on the shoulder or not. The baby, Frasquito, happily collected dirt in his fingers and rubbed it in his hair.

"What happened?"

"I went home about an hour ago. I put the ham on the table and when I turned around, he was there, hissing like the Devil." He said, warming to the tale.

"I was quick. I grabbed him by the tail, and he tried to claw me, but I swung him so fast that he couldn't. I hit his head on the wall. His tongue stuck out. I picked up a chair and beat him with it. There was blood all over the kitchen." He dried his eyes and lit a cigarette. "He had it coming. He really did."

I was stunned. Could this be true? The long, sad story of this beast and his victims coming to an end on such an ordinary afternoon?

"Where is… where is he?" I asked.

"I threw him in the *barranco*," Francisco said, pointing down the track at the bottom of the street. "Do you want to see?"

The three of us went down the stony track to the open ditch where people sometimes threw their rubbish if they thought no one was watching. It was really a shallow ravine, littered with plastic bags and broken furniture and a refrigerator with no door. We looked about for a moment. Francisco poked at a pile of rubbish with a stick, but there was no cat to be seen.

"I threw him right here," he said, wiping the good lens of his spectacles. "I swear it."

We looked for a few minutes and found nothing.

"Are you sure he was dead, Francisco?" I prodded, thinking about the bottle of wine.

"I'm pretty sure I saw his brains," he said grimly. "He was dead, all right."

Twenty years of terror, I thought, and now no body to gloat over.

"One down, " I said, "Eight lives to go."

I don't know exactly when I realised I was going to have to leave Cantilla.

It had come on me gradually. One day the week before a car full of German tourists pulled over next to me on the road. They asked in heavily accented English where to find Cantilla. My heart sank. I shook my head.

"*No hablo ingles*," I lied. As they drove away I experienced a stab of guilt. I thought: *Why did I do that?* If people,

Germans and English and God knows who, were going to find my secret village, they were going to. There was nothing to be done about it. More, there was absolutely nothing I should try to do about it.

On the path one morning I found that I was rehearsing what I was going to say to Bill. One version was casual. It went: "You know, I think maybe Ellen and I will take another job for a while. Earn some money, see some new sights. Come back in a year or so. What do you think?"

Another gambit was more self-conscious: "I've been thinking; we should be doing our bit in Africa, not just hanging around here. You know what I mean?"

But it went deeper than that. My grip on an elusive paradise was starting to yield to reality. There was no place, not even Cantilla, where my longing to come out of alienation, to be *found*, was possible. If I was going to get any sort of inner peace, it would be in the rush and tumble of ordinary events. My events, the events of the modern life Ellen and I had so far led together. Cantilla had indeed almost proved a village too far for our relationship. It had become almost, but not quite, home. I had a sense that we had come perilously close, and, even though things could still be fixed, our relationship was working without a net. But I drew back from telling Bill all this. I wished I didn't feel like such a traitor.

In the event, I didn't even have to speak. We were stacking the peeled logs like high noughts and crosses grids, to let the air circulate. They made two high piles, nearly as tall as we were.

"I guess we'll finish this up another time," Bill said.

"What do you mean?"

"Well, you're taking off again, aren't you?" His voice was cheerful.

"I guess I am."

He looked at me, a slight smile playing on his lips. "That's the right thing to do, you know. This place is nice, but you can't make a whole life out of just being here."

"Well, I don't know. But Ellen..."

"She's right."

"She usually is." We sat in the shade and let the sweat dry on our faces. Pretty soon it would be too hot to work, and we would go down and sit in the river.

"Where to, this time?" he asked.

"It's not certain yet, but I think we're going to a part of north Kenya. There's a job working with some Maasai that got split up from the rest of their people."

"And you're going to do...what?"

"I'm not sure, exactly. We'll have to learn Swahili and all that."

In fact it was called a "presence post," a year of living among the poor groups of Maasai that were experiencing trouble with encroachments from other tribes, losing land and water in the process. We would have a Jeep. We would keep our eyes and ears open, and at the end of a year, write a report to the sending agency for recommendations of projects, funding and new personnel.

Ellen had already gotten early approval from the agency. We needed to go for an interview in the United States, in the wilds of Pennsylvania. We would need new clothes and luggage. We could stop off and visit family. Without being aware of it, a note of excitement had crept into my voice. I only realised it when I saw Bill smile.

"What do you say we do a little presence post down by the river? It's getting hot."

I realised that once again I had followed a path attributed to a nameless Irishman: "How do I know what I think until I've heard what I have to say?"

Bill would look after the house. I was to close it up. Ellen had insisted I buy sheets and cover the furniture. It was going to look like a haunted house when we got back. If we got back.

The car was going back to Manuel, who had an idea of cutting the back seat out to make a light truck out of it. It was shocking how easy it was going to be to leave, when I thought how hard it had been to get here. The worst part was going to be saying goodbye to our friends in the village. I was surprised to find that most people already knew. It made me think that we had always been considered a fleeting phenomenon, and that hurt a little. I got a little drunk in the bar one night and just about avoided crying. Nobody seemed to notice.

On the last day, I went up to Bill's. We drank coffee and dangled our feet in the pond. Ever since he and I had known each other, it seemed that one of us was leaving for somewhere else. Our friendship had deepened through the traumas of the last months, and there was little to say. If someone is really close, there is often a lot of silence between you. I was feeling that there must be some final words, some arrangement left to be made, but everything had already been handled. Ellen, of course, had seen to that. So we whiled away the afternoon as we had so many times before.

I had wanted to say goodbye to Aparicio, but Bill said he had gone to harvest some pears from a friend's orchard, and wouldn't be back before dark. I told Bill to give him my regards.

"He had a message for you, too," Bill said. "He said he wants you to bring him a Maasai spear to stick Cantilleros with."

We said goodbye at the road. Not *adios*, which sounded way too final. Just *hasta luego,* as usual. Sadi saw me fifty yards down the hill. She was just being polite.

Chapter Twenty-eight

Let It Rain

Paco Taxista was chipper as we met to leave Cantilla the next morning. I was burdened with a lot of luggage, so we had agreed that he would take me all the way to the Malaga airport. I felt a little furtive as he brought the taxi as near as possible to my house. There were a lot of people to say goodbye to, but I couldn't face it. We crept down the narrow street that leads to the village, and I saw Guisado, whistling cheerfully as he began a new day of larceny at the English peoples' house.

We headed for Cherin in a morning already heavy with the thick air of summer. As we reached the bend above the *vegas*, I said, on impulse, "Pull over here a minute, will you?"

I got out and walked to the crumbling edge of the road. Below me the first rays of sun picked out the river as it flattened in the densely planted fields. A few men were already at work in this critical pass of the agricultural year. I saw several that I knew, and resisted an urge to call out and wave. Almost exactly beneath me was the new greenhouse of Antonio, El Largo's father. The plastic had not yet been added, but it was only a matter of weeks until the great ugly blister appeared on the landscape. A feeling of hopelessness struggled for dominance in my melancholy mood, but I forced it back. Things would go as they were going to go, I realised, and if someday Ellen and I returned to find *invernaderos* huddled thickly in the *vegas*, so be it.

An incident from my past surfaced in my thoughts. It was many years ago, in North Carolina. I had been re-painting a signboard outside my restaurant, clinging to the top of a ladder that rocked each time I moved. The paint I was using was very expensive, special sign paint of a high pigment content. The label had said very plainly not to let it get wet. The sky, in defiance of the weather report, had been darkening all afternoon. I hurried, foreseeing disaster if the storm caught me in mid job.

Just then I saw someone come by. He was a well-known local house painter, retired after the arthritis got him. He was known as Hey Bob. I called out, "Hey, Bob!" and he stopped at the foot of the ladder.

"I think I've got a serious problem," I said. I explained about the high pigment paint and what the label said. I pointed to the gathering rain clouds. He nodded sympathetically. I asked him what he thought.

"You know what I'd do if I was you?" he said.

"No. What?"

He chuckled. "I'd let it rain," he said.

I laughed with him until we both wiped our eyes. He was right. I had enough to do balancing on a ladder without trying to keep the clouds from bursting. And I had enough to do today, starting a new chapter in my life, without trying to make Cantilla act as I thought it should. It had been here, hugging this frail river for a thousand years, through drought, invasion, civil war and famine. It had seen *senoricos* come and go, dictators appear and fade with every season. It could handle a little plastic and a few English holiday-makers. It could even handle me, with my well-meaning but short-sighted vision of what it ought to be. Yes, Cantilla could even survive me.

At that moment, the electronic chimes of the clock filled the valley. It was eleven minutes too early. I was chuckling when I got in the car.

"What's so funny?" Paco asked.

"Let it rain," I said in English.

"What?"

"Nothing."

At the last bend before the long descent to Cherin, a rider was sitting side-saddle in the middle of the road, smoking nonchalantly. I saw that it was Aparicio, and that he was deliberately blocking our way. I got out. Aparicio nodded to Paco, the limit of his courtesy as far as Cantilleros were concerned. He beamed down at me.

"King Arturo," he greeted me. "Every time I see you, you're on your way out."

"I think you're right," I said, stroking his horse's neck.

"What's so good about Africa, that we don't have right here?"

"Work, I guess," I said.

Aparicio snorted. "Cantilleros aren't interested in work. There's plenty to do, if you people would ever get out of bed."

"Maybe." I felt all out of words, and anyway, there was something wrong with my throat. I extended my hand. He took it in a surprisingly mild grip. I gave a little salute and went back to the car. He nudged his horse out of the way.

As we drove past, Aparicio called out something. I couldn't make out his voice, but I knew what he was saying anyway. I had heard it on the first day we met, which seemed so long ago. I can hear it still.

"*Volveras,* Arturo! You'll be back."

The End

Acknowledgements

Those readers who have consulted their Google maps will know that the village I call Cantilla doesn't exist under that name. I changed the details just enough to protect the fast-vanishing privacy of the people who live there. A few years have passed since the events in the book, but Paco Plaza can still be found in his bar, Paco Taxista still ferries passengers to Granada, and Guisado still plies his larcenous trade with unwary home owners.

So thanks to the people of Cantilla for sharing their stories with me. Thanks to Bill, who is an author now living in Venezuela. Special thanks to my friend Steven Appleby for illuminating these pages.

This book was written for Gilly.